Artists Handbooks

Fundraising

the artist's guide to planning

edited by
Susan Jones

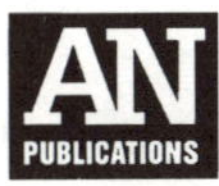

AN Publications

By giving access to information, advice and debate, AN Publications aims to:

- empower artists individually and collectively to strengthen their professional position
- raise awareness of the diversity of visual arts practice and encourage an equality of opportunity
- to stimulate good working practices throughout the visual arts.

Credits

Picture research, Further reading & Contacts Susan Jones

Illustrative examples Susan Jones and Brian Baker (page 34), Alexandra Leadbeater (page 24), Judith Staines (page 46)

Index Susanne Atkin

Proof reader Heather Cawte Winskell (100 Proof)

Cover illustration Yorkshire ArtSpace Society's Environmental Project. *Photo: Julian Quayle* (see page 3)

Design & Layout Neil Southern

Printed Mayfair Printers, Print House, William Street, Sunderland, SR1 1UI

Grant aid AN Publications gratefully acknowledges financial support from the Arts Council

ISBN 0 907730 20 5

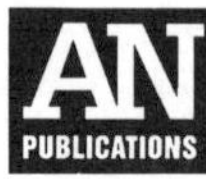

AN Publications is an imprint of
Artic Producers Publishing Co Ltd
PO Box 23, Sunderland SR4 6DG tel 091 567 3589

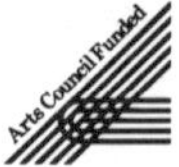

Acknowledgements

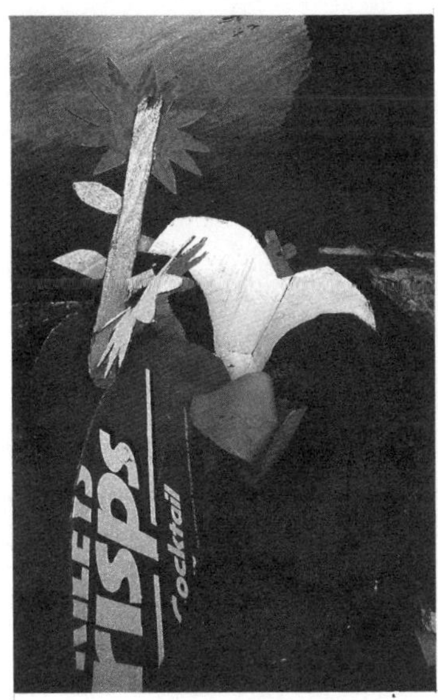

As well as the writers for this book, AN Publications would like to thank the artists and artists' groups who have so willingly contributed information and photographs. We are indebted to the administrators and arts officers whose comments have also made valuable contributions. Val Murray, who read sections of the manuscript whilst in the throes of moving an exhibition from Oldham to Leeds, deserves our special thanks.

Cover image: ***Water lily,* part of a fleet of sculptures made from recycled material for Yorkshire ArtSpace Society's Environmental Week Project with Sheffield schools.**
Photo: Julian Quayle.

Contents

Foreword

Faye Carey
Course Director, MA
Public Art & Design,
Chelsea College of Art,
London Institute

The relationship between art, artists and money is a long and uncomfortable one. This is reflected in the nature of the relationship between artist and patron. The story is told of John Everett Millais who would have the eager dealers assemble in his waiting room, greet them and, drawing on his gloves, would say, "Gentlemen, the pictures are in the studio, the prices on the backs and the butler will show you round." He would then leave them to it.

Artists have long sought to distance themselves from the financial aspects of their work, finding it difficult to promote their work – to put a commercial value – on what is in effect an act of imagination. Hence, there was the rise of the dealer or agent and the promotion of the myth of the artist.

But the attitude of many artists today to what they are doing in the world is changing. There is greater involvement with social and political issues, greater concern about their contribution both to the problems and the solutions. This need to deal with realities, albeit imaginatively, is exposing artists to the challenge of how to get things done themselves, and to learn something about how to evaluate what they do. Ways of getting work funded then becomes an integral part of the creative activity.

Today, we – as artists, arts administrators, art educators – are in the process of trying to foster a more generous, more playful relationship between a citizen and the creative world she or he inhabits by encouraging a wider and more reciprocal role in the imaginative and artistic life of the country: getting more people involved. Artists who wish to meet this challenge need to understand the financial and practical means by which such aims can be achieved. This book, written in the straightforward, thorough and immensely practical style we have come to expect from AN Publications, will help greatly in that understanding.

Introduction

This handbook – aimed at artists, artist-led and other small organisations and others with whom artists work – offers an approach to fundraising which acknowledges the particular role and status of visual artists. Drawing on first-hand experiences and advice, it suggests that successful fundraising results when visual artists develop strategies and techniques which take into account their particular needs and aspirations. It demonstrates that there are many ways to finance exhibitions, travel, workspace, exploration and projects. These range from securing grants from arts boards and charitable trusts to obtaining loans linked with business advice and from gaining patronage to being given subsidised workspace.

Creative artists mix and match these various elements, often using one to lever another or by combining several sources so that, by breaking them down into stages, large-scale projects can be realised. By working in this way, artists are not only able to gain support to make new work but are in a position to change people's perceptions of artists and thereby influence the policies and methods by which visual arts will be supported in the future.

This book shows what can be gained when artists develop the confidence and skills to present themselves as artists rather than – as installation artist Susannah Silver says – "some kind of public relations person or social therapist", and are thus able to unlock sources of money by unlocking the imagination of a potential funder or investor.

1 • Financing your work

Susan Jones There is no ready-to-use 'formula' for fundraising. However, artists seeking ways of funding their practice are more likely to be successful if they apply the same creativity, dedication and attention to detail to their money-raising activities as they do to making art work.

Funding climate

The government's view of the role of the arts, and of artists, is not that they should be considered as a 'special case' – a social necessity and contributors to the quality of people's lives – but regarded merely as another type of business, their success measured against how they benefit the country's economy. As a result, the public funds which are available tend now to be deployed to reward those who are able to show how grants will enable them to increase earned income and also gain sponsorship from businesses or money from other sources. The argument which is often used is that this not only makes public funds go further, but also increases overall funding to the arts by bringing in money from sponsorship, charitable trusts, business development funds or local authority budgets.

The majority of arts activities – whether instigated by individual artists or by groups and organisations – are therefore nowadays expected to be supported by a mixture of public sources linked with private funds. Those involved in the arts are also expected to aspire to being more self-supporting and to show how they will be less reliant on grants in the long-term.

After some fourteen years of such government policies, artists have had to learn to live with the 'enterprise culture' and many have turned it to their advantage. The government Enterprise Allowance Scheme (now also known as Business Boost) has been a stepping stone for some artists and craftspeople, who saw it as a means of breaking out of the trap of being unemployed and feeling they had no status in society. Many have continued being self-employed at the end of the subsidised year, recognising that, despite ups and downs in income, they had greater confidence to put themselves forward, and their ideas subsequently carried more weight with others. Installation artist Susannah Silver describes this as having the power to "present myself as an artist rather than some kind of public relations person or social therapist, and having the ability to persuade people that my art activity has a value in its own right."

Matching funds

Foundation for Sport and the Arts guidelines for applicants describe the items of information they expect to receive in an application:

- Latest financial statements of the enterprise to be assisted
- Description of the purposes for which a grant is sought
- Total cost and amount requested from the foundation
- Statement of how the project will be funded and by whom
- Details such as how many people will benefit from the proposal, numbers of people who can be accommodated in auditorium or spectator accommodation, status of an organisation and who runs it
- Who will be involved in realisation of the plan
- Expression of support for the project from noteworthy sources
- Completed FSA questionnaire

Notably, the word 'arts' is not mentioned in the guidelines, other than in the trust's name.

Although grants for artists are available from arts councils and regional arts boards, competition is fierce, and applications from artists must fit into criteria laid down for particular 'schemes'. Funding bodies usually expect artists to show what combination of sources will be drawn together to fund new work.

For example, Yorkshire & Humberside Arts Board gives grants to individual artists twice a year, with £19,000 available for 1993/94. Twice as many artists usually apply as are successful. The maximum grant is £2000, and applications may be for "any aspect of the production, exhibition, sale or marketing of new or existing work including construction or material costs, equipment, publicity or setting up costs." The board doesn't normally provide more than 50% of the total cost, applicants having to show where the rest will come from. Criteria for assessment include whether the application is clear, concise and well thought out; if the work is innovative and appropriate to context or venue; if exhibition or retail venues have been fixed; how the work will be presented, interpreted or marketed to the public; and whether income and expenditure are realistic. From the date of submitting the application, it will be at least seven weeks before successful applicants will get a cheque. Other schemes include funds to encourage exhibition and presentation of contemporary work, with the priority for 1993/94 being non-Western work, major crafts exhibitions and grants for groups of six or more artists to establish studios or other joint facilities.

Adjusting applications

Fundraising which involves matching or multiple funding inevitably involves working with different sets of criteria, application deadlines and assessment procedures. Artists often have to make applications to organisations whose staff have a limited knowledge of the visual arts and its current trends and terminologies. Each application has also to be adjusted to a particular funder's interests, and paperwork for an application to a regional arts board is rarely suitable for other bodies. For example, selectors for charitable trust funds may not realise that to get an exhibition in a particular gallery is a mark of success unless the application is endorsed by someone whose name means something to them.

It can, however, be frustrating for artists when, having done all the work making different applications to different organisations, they find the possibility of actually doing a project hinges on just one more decision being made in time, or when an important funder vacillates until someone else is prepared to commit themselves.

Sponsorship

The much-vaunted business sponsorship of the arts has made a limited impact on individual artists. Although some have been successful – perhaps gaining free materials or photographic processing for a project – there are relatively few examples of actual cash being handed out. When sculptor Catherine Clover got the offer of a residency in Australia, she approached airlines and other businesses to sponsor her and discovered that many simply are not able to help individuals, although one could give her £500 worth of materials.

Groups of artists have been more successful, with many studio groups, artist-run galleries and artweeks benefiting from sponsorship in kind or in cash. Determination is a key quality, however, as many appeals fall on deaf ears. Reading Artweek sent letters to 1000 companies to get 30 responses worth £11,000 in sponsorship, the voluntary fundraiser spending the equivalent of 20 hours a week over a three-month period to raise their total budget of £25,000 to finance a programme including open studios, exhibitions, residencies and performances.

Juggling

Because of the ways in which money is – and isn't – available to support arts ventures, artists have had to devise imaginative ways of financing their practice. Even a cursory look at the working patterns of visual artists

Basketmaking initiative

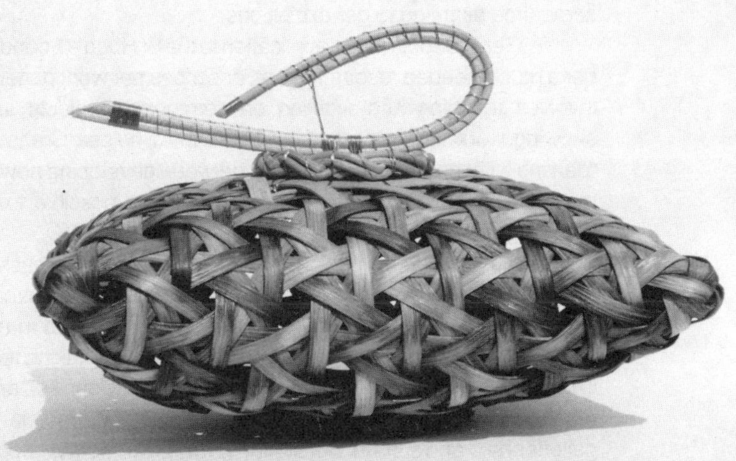

Maggie Henton, ***Pillow Box with Lid*, 1991, dyed cane and wire, 11.5" x 10" x 8". Photo:** the artist

A six-month residency in the North West for basketmaker Maggie Henton grew from the 'New Forms in Willow' conference organised by Projects Environment in 1991. One of three basketmaking and contemporary fibre art residencies set up as the North West Crafts and Environment Initiative by Projects Environment, the aim was to raise awareness of the social and economic history of willow growing and basketmaking locally, and help create a focus for re-assessing the industry's potential value in a region where willow can be grown as a set-aside crop.

As well as running schools' projects and workshops, the artist worked closely with Manchester Metropolitan University introducing basketmaking techniques to the textiles department. This work and other work by Maggie Henton has been helpful in framing guidelines for a new Basketmaking Fellowship being set up by Projects Environment with North West Arts, Cheshire County Council Arts, Lancashire County Council Arts Office and the Countryside Commission as partners.

shows that for most, a 'mixed economy' is the common way of operating. Many combine work in the studio with tendering and applying for commissions and residencies as well as doing bits of teaching, all at the same time as trying to get exhibitions.

Gerry Copp, whose application to the St Hugh's Foundation won her a much-needed research grant, describes her work pattern – which involves teaching and working on community projects as well as showing work through events such as the Chelsea Crafts Fair – as "dealing with the permanent conflict between developing new work and making a living." She does, however, feel it is possible to keep her integrity and earn a living.

Maggie Henton, one of fewer than 30 professional basketmakers in the country, describes her work pattern as "doing [her] usual six hats juggling act." Over the period of a year, she is involved in a range of activities which support and promote her work: undertaking residencies in educational or community settings, working on commissioned pieces, teaching and giving lectures and exhibiting in commercial or public galleries here and abroad. Her strategy is to take and create opportunities as they come, but to concentrate on those likely to make a positive contribution to the development of her work. Although 1993 was mainly taken up with residencies and summer schools, in 1994 she will do little teaching whilst she concentrates on two solo and three major touring exhibitions. "Artists have to be incredibly flexible and do a range of things which contribute to their practice."

Planning

In such conditions, artists need to develop a complex package of skills and attributes. They need not only to be able to assess on a regular basis what they have done, where they are going and the best way of getting there, but also to be prepared to work on several projects, at different stages all at the same time, some of which will be at the ideas stage, others in the first phases of planning and financing, and others in full swing or nearly completed.

Stages

Getting a large project off the ground may seem an awesome task in abstract, but it is more manageable – and has more potential of being funded – if broken down into stages. For example, if you envisage initiating an exhibition to be shown in two years' time, you need to have money not only to produce the body of work (materials, studio costs, subsistence, etc), but also to cover time spent fundraising and promoting the exhibition to prospective galleries. There are also exhibition installation costs (framing, catalogue, display stands, etc) as well as the consideration of your fees and expenses for doing talks, demonstrations and workshops.

Different sources and methods can be used to finance each aspect. For example, you may be lucky enough to cover half the production costs from a regional arts board grant. You may finance studio time from sale of existing work, part-time teaching, undertaking workshops or residencies in the community or perhaps even from a job not related to your practice. Producing 'marketing' information about you and your work to circulate to commissioners, galleries and others could be the subject of an application to a different department of a regional arts board, or it may be of interest to a Training and Enterprise Council whose brief is to help small businesses to promote themselves. Copying or printing costs may be reduced by using local community access print facilities. You may be able to 'barter' with a photographer to get top-quality slides shot of your work in exchange for a piece of your work. A publicly funded gallery should finance all or part of the installation costs either from their own budget or by raising extra money from other sources. It should also pay artists to give a talk if not a fee for exhibiting. Commercial galleries usually offer support in exchange for commission on sales, and, because they have a vested interest in work being sold, work harder to promote it. The 'educational' programme accompanying the exhibition may be of interest to the local authority arts department, educational institutions, sponsors or charitable trusts.

Sculptor Jane Morton from North Shields obtained support in kind from Tyneside TEC, who gave financial and marketing advice for a brochure for her scheme to offer residencies to schools, community groups and businesses in her area. They also covered the cost of colour separations and in return, she gave the TEC a painting. The TEC was "delighted to help. We are sure it will be invaluable in gaining new commissions."

The whole process, from deciding to go for an exhibition to its showing, may take two years if it runs smoothly, or longer if there are problems. You may miss a grant application deadline and have to wait six months for the next. An application to one body may be turned down and you have to send it elsewhere. It may take you a long time to get a new body of work started and to have anything you want to show. The gallery may want to offer you an exhibition but not have a space for twelve months, etc. (In a worst case scenario, you may even find yourself without a studio to make the work in – the landlord having terminated the licence, or the building becoming due for demolition!) Throughout such set-backs, however, your aim is not to lose sight of your objective, to plan and finance an exhibition, even whilst occupied with the various short-term activities such as residencies, teaching, working on a commissioned piece, etc.

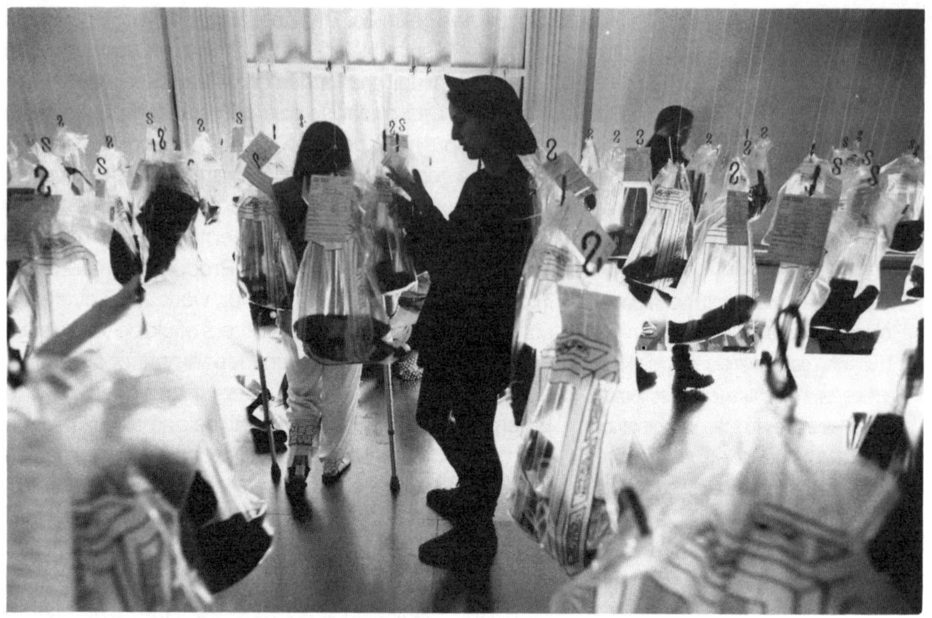

Museum installation, part of the Other People's Shoes project.
Photo: Porl Medlock

In this 'live' artwork, visitors were both observers and the observed as they moved through the display at Harris Museum & Art Gallery, donating or selecting footwear and recording its history.

Speculation and application

An added complication, should one be needed, is that some of these activities are likely to be self-generated whilst others will result from applications for advertised opportunities, or invitations to submit proposals to limited competitions. Whatever the circumstances, opportunities to create new work mean artists will be continuously engaged in documenting work, writing applications to different types of organisations, going for interviews or meetings with clients, as well as informally discussing proposals with potential partners.

Every artist has to find their own 'balance' between speculative proposals and responses to ready-made schemes, as there are advantages and disadvantages to consider. For example, proposals initiated by artists have the potential of being more in tune with their particular interests, although this has to be weighed against time spent on something which may come to nothing.

Foundation for fundraising

Whilst some artists bemoan the amount of time they have to spend on 'administration' because it prevents them from actually creating art, others have come to acknowledge it as being an integral part of being an artist. The Other People's Shoes project – a collaboration between Those Environmental Artists and Impossible Theatre – involved raising £80,000 worth of funds and resources from over 16 organisations including arts bodies, charitable trusts, local authorities and Clarks shoes. The outcome was a year-long series of residencies, workshops, shop installations and events, and exhibitions in Lancashire, West Yorkshire and the East Midlands. The project also included commissions and a publication and plans are underway to make a film. For Val Murray of TEA, "putting over your ideas to raise the necessary money is just another part of the process. Negotiating can be as much a part of engagement and shifting perceptions as anything else."

Susannah Silver also doesn't see a strict division between administration and art making: "The decisions made about typeface on a leaflet or how to approach talking to people about a proposed project are all part of making the artwork and affect the outcome of the work itself."

Practical + creative

In the same way that when a painting is created it combines canvas, paint and brushes with an artist's technical skills, creative thoughts and personal library of artistic experience, establishing effective ways of financing work demands a union between practical and creative elements. Just as a considerable amount of background material has to be gathered, resources located and much thinking done before a painting can even be started, raising money for visual arts projects involves assimilating various elements of 'source material' so that they are ready to be brought into play when needed.

Where you work

Assessing the environment in which you and your work is likely to stand the best chance of flourishing is the first consideration. Even up until a few years ago, it was a commonly held belief that if you wanted to be successful as an artist, you had to go to London and hope a gallery would take you on. Fortunately nowadays, exhibitions – in London or elsewhere – are not now the only way of presenting visual arts to the public and of making an income. As the scope of visual arts has expanded to include art in public, residencies, live art performances, visual arts festivals and other events, every town and city is potentially able to offer something to artists who live there, or who are looking for somewhere to locate.

Inevitably, some parts of the United Kingdom offer more favourable conditions to artists than others. Areas of 'post-industrial' regeneration are often assisted by government funds, some of which filter through to artists. In the past, the Urban Programme scheme funded by central and local government gave grants to some artist-led organisations who could provide activities for the community. Such funds, matched by a sum from Gateshead Metropolitan Borough Council, enabled Malcolm Smith and Steve Marshall to set up Artscope, which provided workshops and encouraged people who are disabled or otherwise disadvantaged to participate in the visual arts. Urban Programme has now given way to City Challenge – another government fund – which 'challenges' inner cities to come up with innovative ways of improving the environment. In Sunderland, this means that the city's glass-making heritage is being highlighted, and a three-year stained glass artist in residence project has been set up as a focus for a long-term developmental strategy for contemporary glass-making. Other such initiatives include appointing a Public Art Development Officer in Middlesbrough to work with community groups, artists, architects and planners to develop projects including residencies and percent for art commissions.

The arts policies of local government, arts councils and arts boards – and therefore the funds they have available to organisations and individuals – affect artists' practice in both the long- and the short-term. They therefore influence the decisions artists make about where to practice, or to whom to make speculative proposals. Having experienced various responses from authorities to her initiatives, Susannah Silver's advice, however, is, "If there isn't any goodwill or sympathy, you might as well forget it!"

In terms of finding out about arts attitudes, local authority unitary development plans are very revealing. Some make no reference to arts at all, whilst others describe policies on public art and uphold the principles of percent for art.

Arts and crafts councils have produced long-term plans outlining their priorities and, as part of the process of becoming ten regional arts boards (from twelve regional arts associations) all have published statements of intent and plans outlining their priorities for the next three years. Such information needs to be gathered and regularly updated by artists, as it forms part of the 'source material' for developing new work, whether in their own location or in other parts of the country.

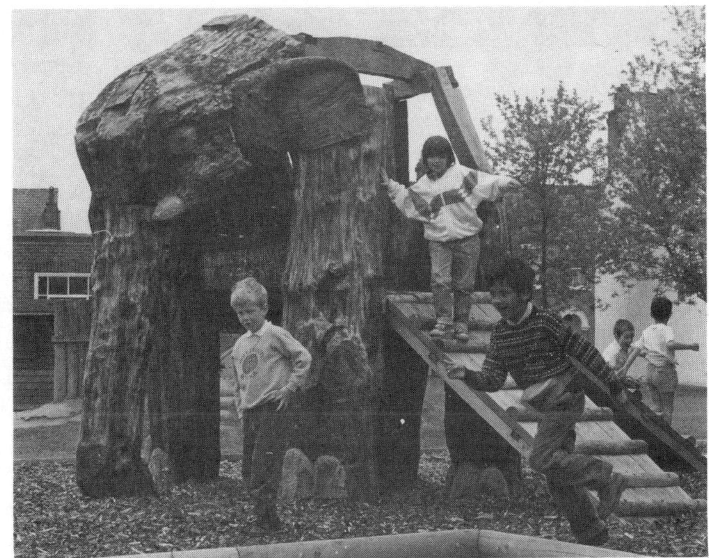

Elephant play sculpture for Holy Trinity Primary School, Merton by Stephen Stockbridge **and** Hannah Littlejones **of Craven Artists Studio Collective. Photo:** the artists

Resources

One factor in determining where to set up – or indeed whether to move on – is whether studio or workshop space is available at an affordable price. Recession and industrial decline in the inner cities means there are often buildings available to be leased out as studios to artists and makers, especially if there is little likelihood of them being used for any other purposes and they are likely to be vandalised if left empty.

Galloway Craft Guild's A4 leaflet contains a map describing 30 members' workshops on a 'craft trail'. Available at Tourist Information Offices, the reverse gives details of crafts available, opening times and the discounts on purchases available to visitors presenting the map!

In rural areas, disused but historically important buildings are often redeployed as craft workshops, the intention being that they will create employment and maintain activity in potentially declining areas whilst at the same time providing something to engage passing tourists. The Rural Development Commission has built some 2800 workshop units for businesses through English Estates, and also provided more than 840 more in partnership with local authorities and trusts. In some parts of the country, it can also provide up to 25% of the cost of converting disused and redundant buildings for new uses including craft workshops.

Disused schools are another potential studio resource for artists. Stephen Stockbridge spent over one and a half years negotiating with the London Borough of Merton to take over a former school kitchen to create space for eight artists and also house a darkroom, workshop and yard area for outdoor work. The Craven Artists Studio Collective aims to

Con-text

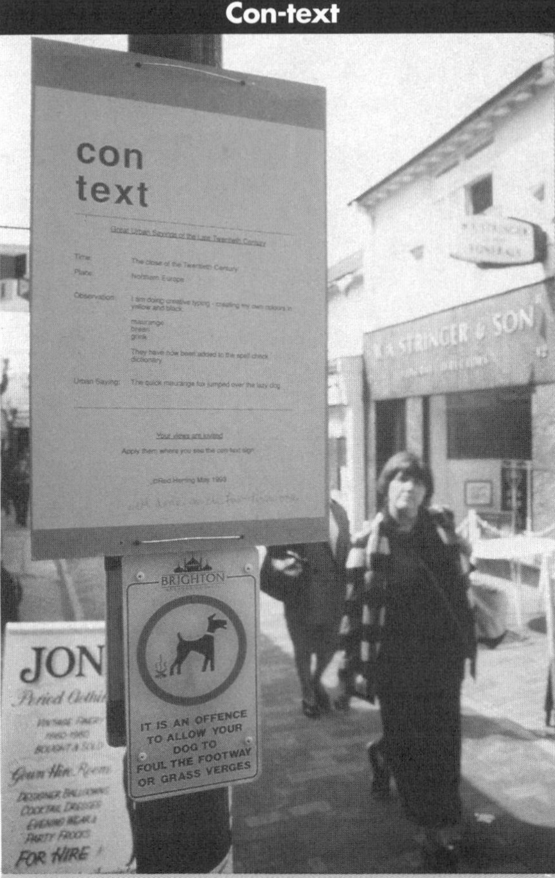

Public notice in the format of a planning notice, part of the Con-text project. Photo: Red Herring

Red Herring Studios has created a strong base for its work in Brighton, despite having moved studios four times in the last ten years. Its programme includes exhibitions, community education activities and art in public spaces projects.

Since 1986, artists have contributed to the Brighton International Festival with projects including the Scaffolding Art Project (temporary outdoor installations and projections), a sculpture trail in the town's public parks and gardens and an exhibition in 1990, 'Crossing Over', showing work by British and East European artists.

The Con-text project was commissioned by the festival for a fee of £3500 to include administration and extra publicity costs. A reaction to the view that festival art is seen primarily as 'visual bunting', it contained text-only images and challenged the boundaries of conventional artwork. Because all works were jointly owned, it virtually got rid of the 'who did what piece?' question.

The 60 hours of meetings between seven artists were regarded as an integral part of defining the artwork, and the collaborative work which emerged was spread over a defined area of shopping and residential streets. Text was applied to 19,000 separate items including carrier bags, sticky labels, serviettes, parking tickets, street signs and other public notices, and two installations. Six radio pieces were also created. All text referred to the visual, and images were unified by being in the colours black and yellow.

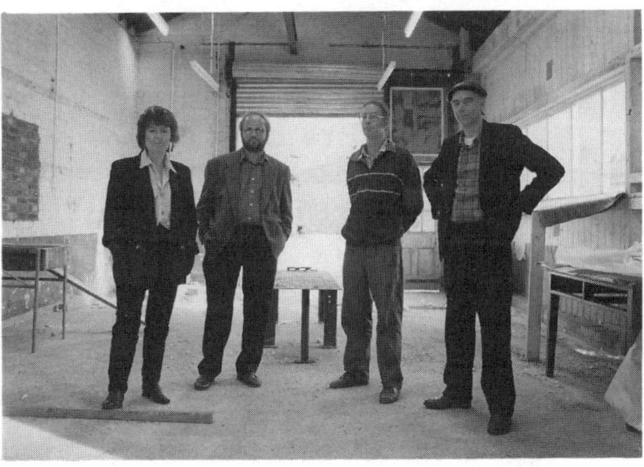

Jenny Freestone, Roger Hatfield, Kevin Storch and Matthew Hilton before work began on converting the print studio at the Maltings. Photo: Barry Thompson

The setting up of Matthew Hilton's studio, where short courses in relief printing will be offered at a low cost, forms part of on-going arts developments for the former brewery site. Others include establishing the Maltings Gallery of Contemporary Art and commission of a sculpture from Kevin Storch.

generate permanent and temporary art in public projects in the borough: "We aim to be an important resource in our area, to contribute and stimulate."

Other conditions which may attract artists to a particular location are whether there are printmaking, photography or sculpture workshops; if there is access to equipment or facilities at cost or subsidised rates (such as woodworking machinery, framing, computers, colour copiers) or the likelihood of being able to show work in galleries, arts centres or other venues. Conversely, the absence, for example, of a printmaking facility in an area may be just the reason to go there and propose setting one up.

As the result of an approach by the artist, property developer Roger Hatfield's company Crossglades Ltd funded conversion of a space into a printmaking studio for Matthew Hilton in the Maltings complex in Hull. For this, a BSIS (Business Sponsorship Incentive Scheme) award was made. In return, Roger Hatfield will be able to select a number of the artist's prints each year. "Matthew was searching for a studio in which to mark his commitment to the city. My pleasure in his work was such that I was delighted to be able to offer him assistance, and I look forward to a long, happy – and proud – association as his patron."

The Crafts Council, recognising the difficulties faced by makers in the first two years of their career, offers a maintenance grant of up to £2500 and 50% of the cost of equipment hire or purchase to a maximum of £5000 to selected makers to establish their first workshop. West Midlands Arts has created a Village Arts Fund to encourage new activities in rural areas which are planned and run by local people and provides between £500-£1000 (up to 50% of the costs), with applications accepted throughout the year.

Building relationships

The third element, perhaps the most important, is to put into place the components which are likely to create a climate for gaining financial support and resources for future work.

As you plan and fundraise for a project, you are making and building contacts with a range of people –

Amongst contacts you may need to build up are:

- arts officers with budgets to which you may apply now or in the future
- people with access to useful resources – equipment, materials, buildings, personnel, etc
- people whose work overlaps with yours – art teachers, community workers, planners and environmentalists
- people who can help promote your work – gallery organisers, press and media reporters, marketing consultants
- people who can recommend you and your work to others – councillors on arts committees, respected local people
- potential purchasers or commissioners: architects, local business people, healthcare institutions.
- people with skills and experience you need – business advisers, etc
- other visual artists whose work and work practices have a similarity with or are complementary to yours

arts officers, business people, teachers, architects, community workers, etc. As you write applications, you are testing out and refining ways of describing yourself and your work, and devising ways of capturing people's imagination and appealing to their particular needs and interests. You are also getting to know people who may, for example, be able to give you access to equipment or space, best price printing and copying facilities, help with planning and raising money for a project, sources of information on grants and other kinds of support. These people are valuable, not just for the project in hand, but for others you may want to do in the future.

Thus, more important than finding the correct name and title of the person who will look at a grant application is realising your best interests are served by building up productive relationships with those key individuals, the aim being to raise their awareness of the visual arts in general, and gain respect for your work in particular. Sculptor Jane Morton – who graduated from Liverpool Polytechnic in 1990 and moved to the North East to set up her studio and initiate her own commissions and residencies – has found that to make one out of five applications or proposals successful depends on making these kinds of personal contacts and in nurturing potentially beneficial relationships.

Getting to know relevant arts officers – in arts councils or boards and local authorities – is particularly important. These people are not only concerned with administering grants. They are also involved in assessing whether their organisation's current policies are working, and also in advising their superiors on the development of future arts policies, including the ways in which they support artists.

Two-way process

Building relationships with people who are directly or indirectly involved in the visual arts and raising their awareness of the value and social significance of what artists do is far too important to be left to others. Presenting yourself and your ideas in person – so that the integrity and purpose of your work is not diminished by interpretation – may sometimes seem an overwhelming task. However, learning how to convince other people they should work with you to realise your concept will not only ensure you get funds to do it, but also give you a real sense of achievement. As a result, it is more likely that the project will be successful.

More importantly though, the status of artists will have been raised in the eyes of people who, by coming to respect what artists contribute, will be far more willing to support visual arts initiatives – yours and other artists' – in the years to come.

2 • Developing a strategy

Maureen Mackin

Very often, successful fundraising comes down to good planning. Nobody can win every time, but you stand more chance if you have formulated a framework within which to set your goals and deadlines. For some artists, the idea of a 'strategy' may take some coming to terms with. It can smack of artificiality, contrivance, conspiracy and the laying down of something too cold and objective by far for creative people.

There's always the fear that formulation of strategies could put an end to the pattern of artistic endeavour as we know it: gone the thrill of gaining that elusive once-in-a-decade bursary, the frenetic activity to produce new work, get reports written and set up exhibitions all within the deadline year. Instead, the horror of five-year plans – multi-pronged campaigns directed at all appropriate organisations, acquisition of books on marketing, strategic planning, managing finances and exporting to Europe.

Strategy = Creativity

In fact, formulation of a well-thought-out strategy could be one of the most creative and ultimately useful things that you ever do. That visual artists have a contribution to make to society which is made more difficult by inadequate resourcing is undeniable, and although we would like to see better government funding of the arts, the reality is that resources are and will continue to be scarce.

In such an environment, it is better to try to take control of your own future – be proactive rather than passive. When it comes to creating conditions more likely to provide you with a regular income, formulation of a fundraising strategy is imperative. Crises will inevitably still arise, but you should be better able to cope with them – to 'manage' them, rather than have them manage you.

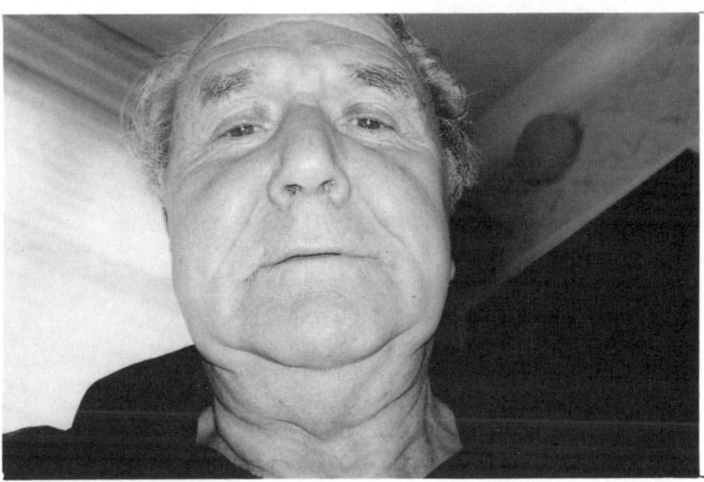

From a self-portrait project, supported by Photo Works North. Photo: Charlie Toal

Photo Works North is dedicated to the promotion of photography in Northern Ireland. Recognising that planning begins with an analysis of the environment, they carried out a survey of the needs of members and other interested individuals. They obtained funding from the Northern Ireland Voluntary Trust to carry out a market research study. Questionnaires were distributed throughout Northern Ireland to individuals, galleries, arts centres and trade outlets. The results of the survey will be fed into future policy-making.

Overall plan

A fundraising strategy is not something to be developed overnight. It requires much thought and needs to be an integral part of a bigger developmental plan. A strategy is the planning and directing of the whole operation of a campaign which will enable you to finance your work now and in the future. It should aim to cover the projects and ventures you want to do in the next six months as well as those you want to accomplish in the next two, three and four years.

Developing a fundraising strategy is not just a case of gaining the skills to write a funding application, or being able to raise the funds for a one-off project. Although both are valuable, their meaning and potential are heightened when they become parts of an overall plan. Such a strategy will provide you with a framework within which you can make considered choices. For example, it will help to decide which opportunities you apply for and which ventures you can afford to develop speculatively, whether to join with others to set up a workshop, or whether to move to premises with exhibition or display space.

Self-analysis

The first step in formulating a long-term strategy or developmental plan is to take a long look at yourself. This means assessing your career to date, achievements, things that have not gone well and, importantly,

Face Fits

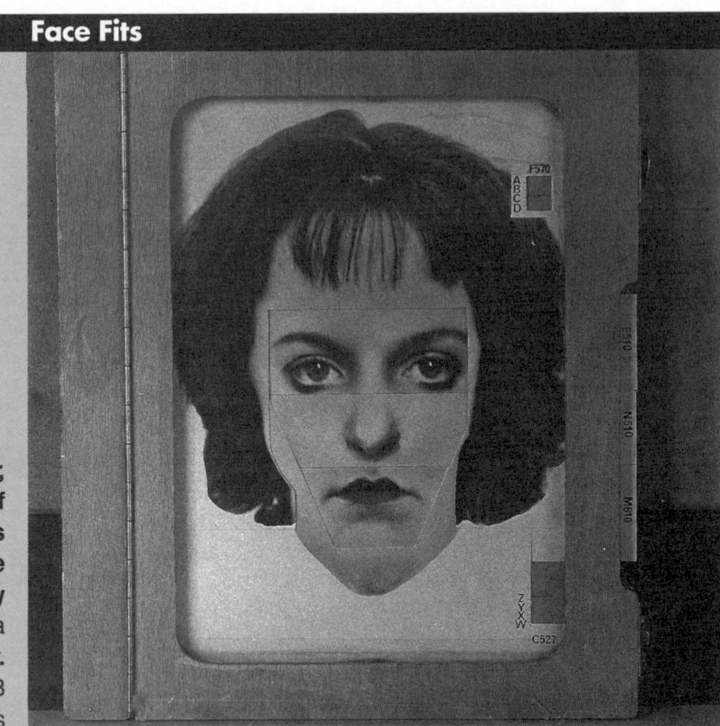

***The Stranger*, from a series of six self-portraits using police photo-fits by** Alexandra Leadbeater. **Photo:** PC B Jones

I have been self-employed for over ten years, precariously supporting myself from sales of paintings and part-time work. Financial insecurity made it difficult to work consistently. My life was completely changed, however, by an exchange visit to Brazil in 1991 funded by Southern Arts. I was able to spend my entire time making art and, more importantly, thinking about art. This liberating experience reinforced the view that I wasn't satisfied with making pictures with the primary concern of selling them. I began to feel more interested in making events, perhaps involving other people, which could have commercial spin-offs.

When I finally got back to Britain, I was in a worse financial situation than before, because having returned to Brazil twice after the exchange period for exhibitions I had organised, I was still paying off the airfares. Faced with the choice of giving up or going for it, I decided to set up a project with plenty of scope for public involvement and which would get my name known and lift me from the depths of obscurity.

As there are few chances for artists to exhibit, I was encouraged to make my own opportunity. I took the idea of making an exhibition of myself to extremes with an exhibition called 'The Face Fits'. The main aim was to fulfil all guidelines for grant aid and business sponsorship and to attempt to cover all the politically correct criteria for a public exhibition – involving the local community and schools, collaborating with other artists and running participatory workshops.

I was given a £1000 grant by the Milton Keynes Foundation to develop the idea of presenting a series of images of myself using police photo-fit, with a competition run for people to try to recognise me from the pictures. As the earliest exhibition slot at the Exhibition Gallery in Milton Keynes was in 1994, I was delighted when my proposal to run the project in Middleton Hall – in the heart of Milton Keynes shopping centre – during Bucks Art Week in June 1993 was accepted. The initial idea of the project was expanded to include likenesses of me by several artists and more than 50 other portraits by artists selected after an advertisement in *Artists Newsletter.*

I had less than six months to plan and organise the project. I hadn't realised how long things could take to get going and there were many worries and frustrations. The Shopping Centre immediately gave £4000 sponsorship, and the next step was to find commercial sponsors and people to participate.

Luckily, I found Sally Lewis to co-ordinate the project who, although she had no previous experience, shared with me tasks such as drawing up budgets, raising sponsorship, and liaising with artists and bureaucrats. All this went on whilst I was trying to make my own work and against the background of a constantly-ringing telephone.

We wrote more than 100 letters to anyone we thought might be interested in the project selecting, for example, any companies from the *Yellow Pages* whose name included the word 'face'. The range of people embraced beauticians and brain surgeons. A main aim was that the exhibition would contain something of interest for everyone, and I also didn't want people to be intimidated by the idea of an art exhibition.

Most of the companies approached for sponsorship in kind seemed to be suffering from sponsorship fatigue. We got few replies to the letters and became adept at spotting the word 'unfortunately' before hopes were raised. It was incredibly difficult to persuade people to take part, despite the huge numbers who would pass through the exhibition. One reason was because, ironically, in a venue in the heart of the shopping centre, no direct selling is allowed. I had wanted the space to be full of hairdressers and beauticians offering people the chance to change their image as well as providing space for working artists. In addition to six artists running paid workshops, only two others could be persuaded to do quick portrait sketches without guarantee of sales, and I was disappointed there weren't more commercial participants.

Companies who did contribute were very generous. Canon provided a colour laser photo-copier for the week for public and schools workshops. Two photo-booths were lent with free services, plus several computers and appropriate software. Local businesses did demonstrations of hair styling and make-up. Other companies gave prizes and card, with Liquitex donating paint and brushes. Money raised from face painting workshops went to the charity Changing Faces who had a stand in the exhibition.

The project's overall budget was £10,500. The Milton Keynes Foundation gave a further £1000, Southern Arts gave £2000 and, a week before the show, £2500 came from Milton Keynes Marketing. Administration costs were more than we budgeted and Sally Lewis continued to work on the understanding she would be paid in paintings if there wasn't enough money. Administering the project turned into a full-time job for both of us, and we therefore couldn't make any other income.

It was a nail-biting six months. I was constantly worried that any financial deficit would fall on me personally. We kept trimming costs and, as a consequence, the show was compromised. If we had known the total income at the outset, we would have felt more in control and everything would have been easier. It is possible to demand quality service from firms when you can pay for it, but if you have to rely on in-kind sponsorship, you have to accept what they offer.

So often at an exhibition the artist is the last person anyone talks to or can identify. With over 50 images of my face, it was difficult to miss me and I got a very positive response from the public. At least 2000 people a day passed through the six-day exhibition. People enjoyed getting dressed up and getting a free photo from the booths. Images could be manipulated by the computer or enlarged on the copier, and nearly everyone went home with an image of some sort.

deciding where you would like to be in, say, five years' time. The means by which you will get to where you want to be will be your strategy.

Since survival depends upon acquiring sufficient funds to get by, your strategy for development must incorporate the framework and mechanisms to access that money as well as any sponsorship in kind and other resources. The key is planning.

Pain of planning

Some people were born to plan whilst others seem positively allergic to it. This is evident in all walks of life. Although it can be a disconcerting prospect, it does bring you face-to-face with reality: you are forced to step aside from situations and you may be surprised at the potential solutions which arise when you look for a long-term view.

Once you have dealt with the first step of self-analysis, you will be better able to confront, come to terms with and plan for tricky situations in the future.

Comparisons with business

The business world devotes substantial resources to planning and strategic thinking. Such activities employ numerous business executives whose job it is to take a long hard look at their organisations and the individuals in them, examining what one each does and how they relate to each other as well as to the business overall. Such people also examine the external environment too, doing market research and mounting promotional campaigns. The generation of sales and profit depends upon the 'world' of their organisation connecting with the 'world' outside.

Based on their research, new products are launched on the market, unpopular ones taken off, customer services improved, or new pieces of equipment bought to keep them in line with the competitors, and so on. Without self- and environmental analysis and the resulting formulation of strategy, companies would go out of business.

Artists and artist-led organisations can use some of these methods and adapt them to their particular circumstances. In setting out to appraise your work, relevant questions might be:

- What is the purpose of your work?
- Who and where are the audience and markets for it?
- What are your objectives and goals?
- Have you achieved any of them, and if not, what prevented you from doing so?
- What are your strengths and weaknesses?
- Are you in the right location?

- What equipment do you have – is it used effectively?
- What are your current financial resources?
- What would additional funding enable you to do?
- What's going on in the outside environment – locally, nationally, internationally – which is relevant to your work?
- What are the current national and regional policies for the arts and crafts?
- What are other artists and craftspeople doing – could you collaborate with them?

A lot of common sense is involved in this type of analysis and in projecting future activities. None of us exists in a vacuum and it is increasingly important for visual artists to inform themselves about what is going on around them and maximise their potential, both as creative people and in a community context.

In devising a plan, take into account your individual needs and aspirations as a creative artist, plans to involve yourself in projects with other artists or with the community, possible periods of part-time teaching, travel, exhibitions, residencies, exchanges, involvement in publications, and so on.

Use the freedom of self-employment to your advantage. Being better informed means you will be one step ahead or at least prepared for whatever problems or opportunities may arise.

Planning is about:

- self-evaluation – identifying strengths and weaknesses
- setting objectives – ie specific and measurable outcomes, and goals, both short- and long-term
- formulating alternative/intersecting programmes of action – flexibility is sometimes the key to survival
- getting to know your potential funding environment – grant-aid available, employment opportunities, percent for art schemes, etc
- devising mechanisms to monitor your progress.

Funding environment

The funding environment nowadays is much more varied than even a decade ago. Although the possibilities of selling work or obtaining a grant from an arts funding body still exist, as artists began to realise the advantages of engaging with communities, funding and employment opportunities have increased. These include working with local authorities, through percent for art schemes, with private sector sponsorship, in

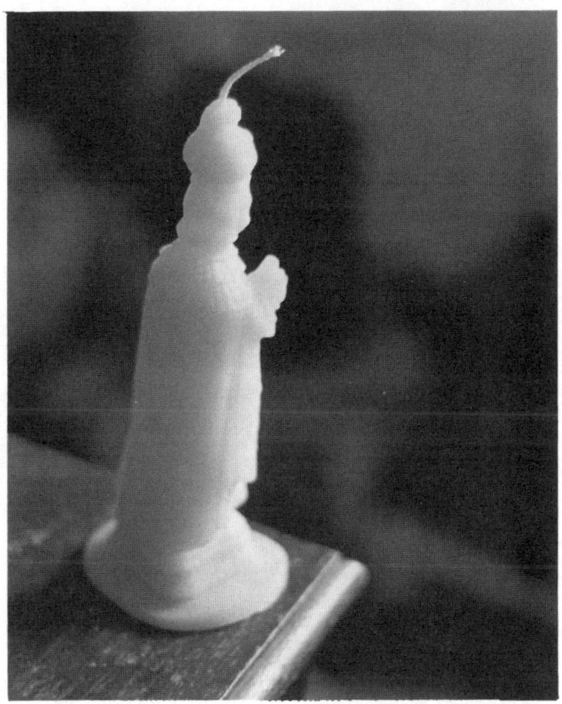

Image by Mark Orange **for the cover of the 'Presentense' catalogue.**

A group of young Belfast artists – the 6 into 18 Group – work together to create opportunities to show their work in non-gallery spaces. During 1992, they organised exhibitions in Belfast and Derry and also ran a series of lectures in Belfast's Old Museum Arts Centre and Arts Council Gallery. These activities were based on a great deal of voluntary work by the artists. Their latest exhibition, 'Presentense', which took place in a Belfast city centre shopping mall in Summer 1993, however, secured funding from the Arts Council of Northern Ireland, enabling them to produce a substantial exhibition catalogue.

healthcare groups, schools, libraries and more recently, through the opportunities and exchanges with other European countries.

It does not follow, however, that resources are plentiful for visual artists, because whilst new opportunities have grown up, government funds have effectively decreased. The development of information resources (magazines, databases, artists' registers, etc) has increased competition for the funds available to artists. It is therefore crucial that an artist develops an effective fundraising strategy, based on their particular needs and aspirations.

Long-term plan

When a company refers to its 'business plan', it is referring to a document which gives a set of projected figures summarising planned activities showing income (from sales, fees, government grants, etc) and expenditure (on raw materials, transport, salaries, telephone, electricity, etc) for at least the next three years. With public arts funding being as precarious as it is, many arts organisations now operate on a year-to-year basis, with the unfortunate result that long-term planning is discouraged.

35 King Street Gallery

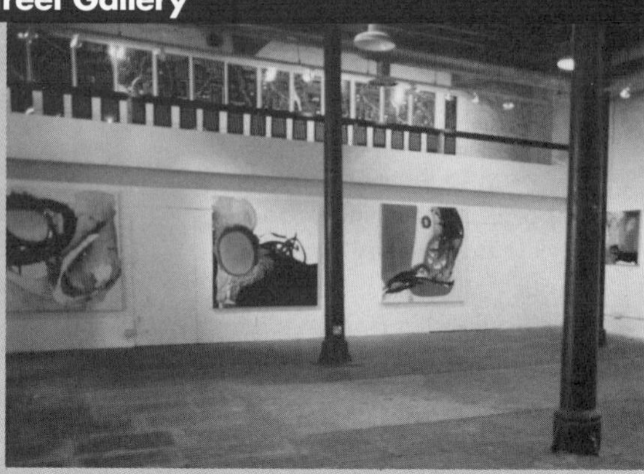

Installation at 35 King Street Gallery. Photo: Artspace Bristol

The aim for Artspace Bristol in setting up an artist-run gallery space as an adjunct to their studios and community outreach activities was to provide a focus for a wider group of artists and get more art work out into public view as well as helping to create networks, spread information and improve opportunities for artists.

The gallery, modelled on artist-run galleries such as Transmission in Glasgow and Castlefield in Manchester, was set up initially at 27 Colston Street in May 1992, and moved to 35 King Street in March 1993. A steering committee, including representatives from Arnolfini, University of West of England, the African and Asian Visual Artists Archive and local artists, was set up to develop the gallery and ensure it gained access to existing resources and networks.

It took nine months to raise £2500 from an appeal to local businesses to make contributions to setting up and the first year's exhibition programme. This was matched by a £3000 grant from South West Arts from whom Artspace already receives project funding towards administration and programme costs. Architects who lease the building subsidise the ground rent, leaving the gallery to pay £170 a month towards overheads and £50 a month business rates.

A membership scheme has been launched to get more people involved in the gallery, and, in the future, to provide volunteers to invigilate exhibitions. "Priorities are to show work which would not otherwise be seen, give less experienced artists an opportunity to show their work and ensure a good mix of artistic styles and media. This is a self-help gallery and artists are expected to arrange invigilation, give talks and prepare and send invitations out to their own contacts and to the gallery's own mailing list. The cost of this and sending out press releases are the only charges we make."

Although direct comparison with the business world may at times seem inappropriate because many arts activities are non-commercial, an alternative view is that an arts organisation receiving funding from a single source – a regional arts board revenue grant for example – is like a business with only one customer. Making contingency plans against losing that 'customer', and moving towards a 'mixed' funding base are issues which must be dealt with and which evolve through the planning process.

For individual artists, dependency upon the prospect of an arts council or regional arts board grant is neither realistic nor desirable. Even if you have been successful once or even twice, you won't be every time. A grant should be viewed as just one of a range of options which exist. For example, an artist may initiate projects in collaboration with other artists or groups in the community, undertake residencies in hospitals, schools and libraries and sell work through exhibitions or fairs. Craftspeople often do all these things whilst also making one-off items to commission, participating in national and international crafts fairs, and teaching on further and higher education courses.

An effective fundraising strategy is one which takes all these potential sources into account, mixing and matching them as appropriate. For example, sales from an exhibition may finance a European visit to recharge the batteries and develop new work, or a part-time teaching job provide the income needed to edition a series of prints for an exhibition.

Sources of support

As well as selling work, income from teaching and other arts-related activities, there are many other sources of support from which visual artists may benefit. However, not all the following list can provide cash. Methods of support may include rates relief, subsidised rent, access to resources or equipment, interest-free loans and help with distributing publicity.

Those worth investigating are:

Local authority

- Recreation & Arts, Tourism & Leisure, Amenities, etc
- Libraries & Arts
- Parks & Cemeteries
- Architects
- Planning
- Social Services

- Education
- Public Works
- Public Health
- Economic Development – may include City Challenge in some areas

Other sources

- Arts councils – England, Scotland, Wales, Northern Ireland and Ireland
- British Film Institute
- Charitable trusts
- Crafts councils – England and Ireland
- Department of Trade & Industry
- European funding sources
- Health authorities
- International trusts
- Regional arts boards – England
- Rural Development Commission
- Sponsorship
- Tourist boards
- Trades unions
- Training & Enterprise Council (England), Local Enterprise Council (Scotland), Local Enterprise Development Unit (Northern Ireland)
- Urban development agency
- Urban development corporations

Where to look

The Further reading section lists the many directories and source books where details of agencies, trusts and potential business sponsors can be found. There is no need, however, to buy all the books, as main libraries should have reference copies of the most important ones. Resource centres run by voluntary sector agencies usually have them too.

Networking

See 9 • Contacts

Faced with a vast amount of information, short-cuts are welcome. Taking advice, from people who have specialist knowledge about fundraising techniques or those responsible for giving out money, cuts down the time you would otherwise have to spend researching the policies and priorities of potential funders and matching them to your project ideas.

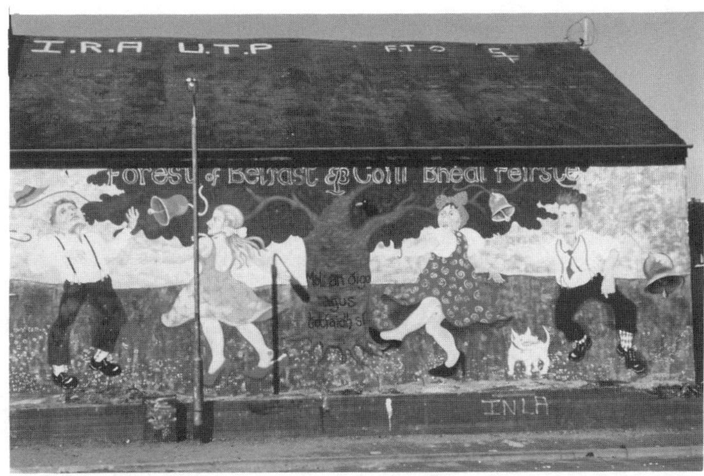

Rita Duffy, *Forest of Belfast (Lower Ormeau Road, Belfast)*. Photo: Mark Johnson

A Belfast artist well-known for her involvement with community arts projects was asked to co-ordinate a multi-site mural project. Funding was obtained from the Arts Council of Northern Ireland's community arts department with sponsorship in kind coming from a local paint company. Getting to know 'who did what' on the sites provided opportunities to request assistance from local builders, the local housing authority, city council and property developers, some of whom provided help.

As voluntary organisations rely almost totally on self-raised funds, it is worthwhile making contact with those in your area. You may be able not only to make use of their contacts and fundraising experiences, but also develop collaborative projects with them, and subsequently tap into sources of funds which might otherwise be unavailable to you.

If you are unsure about your fundraising skills, there are opportunities to learn more about how to do it through courses and seminars.

Research

Personal contacts made ahead of submitting an application help you to find out if your objectives, goals and needs are in line with those of potential funders. As trusts tend to have well-defined remits, it is essential to find out if their interests extend to your projects. In assessing which bodies to approach, as well as their policies and priorities, find out about size of grants, any geographical, age or other limitations, application procedures and deadlines. Some trusts and companies can't fund individuals but can assist groups, whilst others can only give grants to organisations with charitable status.

For large-scale fundraising ventures, it may be necessary to form a group or association and, for long-term projects which need substantial public or trust funds, to gain charitable status. There are, however, advantages and disadvantages to take into account, notwithstanding the legal costs and the time it takes to gain approval from

Spaghetti Junction

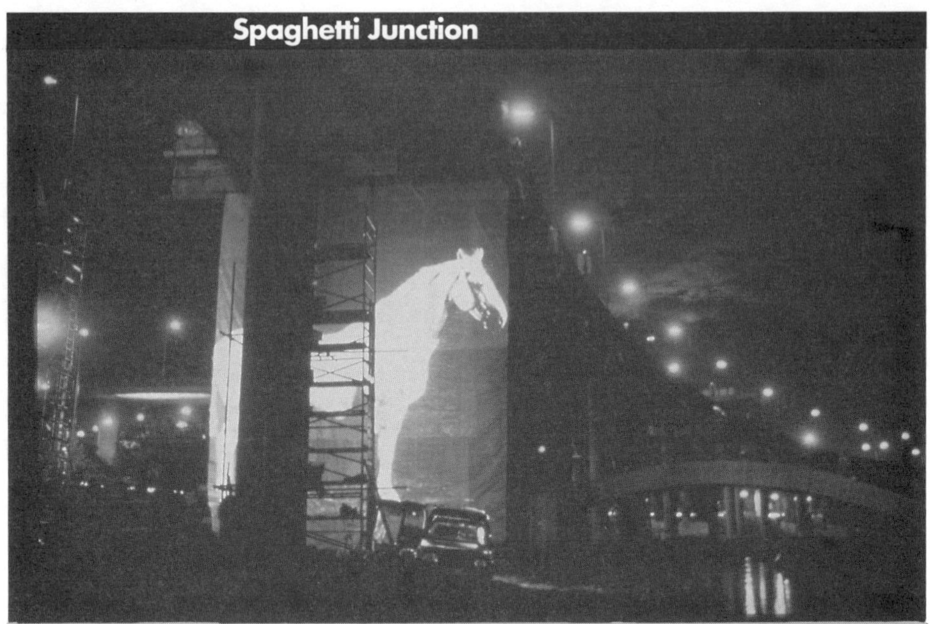

***Colossus,* a monument video projection under Spaghetti Junction by** Colin Pearce. **Photo:** © Kate Green & Fine Rats International

Fine Rats International had already built a reputation for exciting innovation when they conceived an exposition to be staged under the Gravelly Hill Interchange – better known as Spaghetti Junction – to coincide with the structure's 25th anniversary. After securing an Arts Council research grant worth £5000 in the winter of 1991/92, the group – Francis Gomilla, Colin Pearce, Ivan Smith and Mark Renn – were able to travel, attend festivals and plan out the daunting fundraising and technical challenges inherent in the project. Research work in 1992 was assisted by their success in securing a £3000 grant from Birmingham City Council to supplement the Arts Council money.

Initially, they were envisaging a budget of £80,000. In the end it was close to £100,000. However, Colin Pearce points out. "The scale and complexity was such that it might well have been £200,000." Indeed, some of the negotiations with invited visiting artists proved tense because, Pearce believes, they couldn't believe the budget for such an ambitious event stretching over a 34-acre site wasn't larger.

It happened on two successive evenings in early September 1993. Pearce recalls, "It was Russian roulette as we only finally secured the last £40,000 of it four weeks before we did the exhibition." This was private sector sponsorship from companies new to the arts, thus levering Business Sponsorship Incentive Scheme (BSIS) money.

The Arts Council had been the first port of call. The detailed project proposal went to them in late 1992. Pearce says, "Our applications are full of strong visual images with text which argues exhaustively for the central theme though not, critically, at great length." Their approach has worked well. Shortly before obtaining a £25,000 project grant for Spaghetti Junction the group were approved for three-year franchising for core costs at £20,000 a year. A great deal of the 1993 money under-pinned the project.

The Arts Council grant helped to bring in West Midlands Arts, who contributed £11,000 in all from its Film, Production and Visual Arts budgets. Of the regular private funders the Paul Hamlyn Foundation came in with £5000. The bulk of the rest of the money came from first timers, hence the BSIS input and the EC funds.

Smith and Pearce pay tribute to the support of MEP Christine Crawley in the process of securing EC money, a £15,272 grant from the Kaleidoscope Programme. This is a 4 million ecu a year fund which receives applications from organisations across Europe.

Under Spaghetti Junction was conceived as a European project. All invited artists were from Europe, though not all from member-state countries. Pearce emphasises the fundraising importance of that, "The two things we used as a hook were the site and the international importance of the exhibition."

Fine Rats International perceive difficulty in raising funds for big projects from large companies. "By the time we had the Arts Council grant it was much too late to obtain support from large corporate donors," says Pearce. He doubts that public funds are ever likely to be committed more than 9-12 months ahead, however. They are not optimistic that a way round this can be found. Smith says, "Our credentials were only strong enough once we had the Arts Council money." Unfortunately, this was way past the big players' deadlines.

In addition to the money from new sponsors Ericson and Science Cosmic, the group obtained discounted prices for equipment and help in kind. Without this, the exhibition would have had to be cut back. Notcutts, for example, broke one of their cardinal rules and lent Ivan Smith live plants for one of his artworks. The artists have become skilled at negotiating strange requests with suppliers. Their advice to artists new to this is simply "approach people cold and ask them for what you want."

For a large project, the financial backing has a key secondary benefit too. The group had a difficult relationship with the Department of Transport throughout the process, but each time they secured a new backer, it persuaded department officials to drop objections.

the Charity Commission. First of all, working as a group inevitably slows down decision-making processes. Also, the rule that a trustee cannot benefit financially from their charity means that artists who want to undertake work for the group (commissions, residencies, etc) cannot be trustees, and therefore have to hand management and decision-making of their organisation to other people. Amongst advantages are that charities can obtain tax and rates relief and, overall, may be viewed more sympathetically by potential donors than organisations who aren't.

In search of partners

If you pursue European funding, a great deal of groundwork must be done in advance. European-funded projects usually require the engagement of at least one 'trans-national' partner, that is an organisation from another member state willing to collaborate with you. Potential partners need to be researched well in advance of making an application as their participation must be rationalised and budgeted for in any proposal.

More artists now find and create opportunities to travel abroad, using visits to make contacts with like-minded people and others with skills or facilities useful for future collaborative projects. It is important that such valuable information is stored, for use both by the artist themselves and also if possible to be available to others. For example, artists in studio groups or collectives could collate lists of contacts and other details on index cards or on a computerised database and offer it as a resource to other artists in the area.

Fundraising plan

Whether you are an individual artist or a small visual arts organisation, the starting point is the same. You must:

- define yourself, aspirations and needs
- formulate aims and objectives and methods of achieving them
- draw up a long-term plan of, say, 3-5 years but with six-month short-term plans within that time-scale
- set financial targets and prepare realistic budgets
- set your own deadlines
- make appropriate applications for funding.

An example of how this could apply to an individual artist or craftsperson might be: planning a year's travel in year one, making a body of new work in year two, setting up an exhibition which includes catalogue and

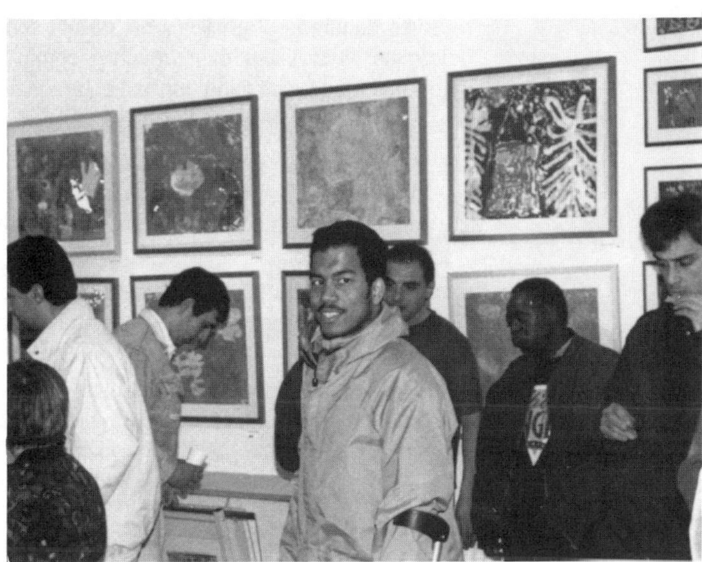

Sara Clark **with work in progress for the 'Artists First' exhibition. Photo:** Hardware Gallery

Hardware Gallery mounted 'Artists First', an exhibition of work by 21 artists from North London who are all young adults with learning difficulties. Their work had been made at North East London College and Ormond Road workshops under the guidance of artists Freddie Robbins, Adam Sutherland and Sarah Thomson. The exhibition was sponsored by Sainsburys plc, The Mercers Company, Quicksilver Messenger Service and Starsigns. Proceeds from sale of work went towards maintaining workshops and courses for artists with disabilities.

educational workshops in year three, developing a residency for year four and moving to a larger workshop in year five.

During each year, three months might be spent doing part-time teaching, three days a month on setting up contacts and networking, following up leads, reading art magazines and publications to keep up to date, etc and two days a month might be spent actively pursuing sales or possible commissions. Thinking and operating in this way will take a little discipline, but will pay off in time.

By checking your activities against a monthly budget – expected income offset by expenditure – it will become clear where you need to defray shortfalls with additional fundraising.

Fundraising applications

Some funding bodies have application forms but many don't. The skills you gain from making proposals will therefore stand you in good stead for putting together your own application. Success will lie in your ability to engage the funder's imagination and convince them that they should entrust their money or other resources to you. Ask yourself what you would look for in an application if you were the administrator who often receives hundreds of applications, and in some cases may have to determine which ones even reach a committee for selection. The guidelines for a fundraising application are that it should:

- define your project clearly – don't assume the reader will understand the need for it
- outline your track record as an individual or as an organisation – if a first project, include references and declarations of interest from appropriate people
- formulate specific, measurable and attainable objectives, goals and deadlines, showing how you will evaluate and report back on the project
- prepare budgets allowing for all costs – if a long-term project, estimate costs for future years with allowances for inflation
- ask the funding body for an amount in keeping with what they usually give – don't ask for £5000 if the maximum grant they give is £500
- if appropriate, isolate a particular item which you think might fit their remit, for example a piece of equipment, series of workshops, etc.
- include all sources of other funds and other expected income and indicate if confirmed
- present your application well
- be confident, convey the sense of personal commitment and enthusiasm which motivated you to create the project in the first place
- test out your application by getting comments from someone whose opinion you value and who has had some success with fundraising themselves.

Timing

Fundraising is a time-consuming process – formulating an overall strategy, preparing applications, waiting for results and so on. Although it depends on the size of the project, you should usually allow 6-9 months for adequate preparation. For large projects, it is usual to plan at least 18 months in advance. Time is needed because:

- some organisations have fixed cycles for considering applications
- popular sources are generally over-subscribed and an application may have to wait several months to be considered
- local businesses may need to refer to regional or head office
- local authorities can't allocate funds until budgets are agreed, and applications generally go to committees of councillors

- no-one ever seems to have any funds left between November and March if their financial year ends on April 5!

By starting your fundraising well in advance, if an application is rejected by one funder, you still have time to submit it to another.

It is also useful to liaise with others working in the visual arts to ensure you are not duplicating or competing by applying to the same bodies at the same time.

Feasibility studies

See also 7 • On the receiving end

If your project is on a particularly large scale and will have a substantial budget, it is often wise to seek 'seed' funding for an initial or pilot study to check the project's 'feasibility'. Although a relatively new concept in the arts, the advantage of a feasibility study is that it shows whether a project needs to be modified to maximise its potential, or indeed, whether it won't work at all and should be abandoned. The Prince's Trust Go & See scheme, which enables artists to go to another European country and make contacts and develop a project, is an example of how to finance a feasibility study.

Feasibility studies can be useful and economical exercises, advantageous both to you and your funders. They serve to increase your confidence in being able to carry out the project within the parameters you outlined to funders whilst at the same time they will increase their confidence in you.

Funding in stages

See also 1 • Financing your work and 6 • Alternatives & opportunities

For a large-scale project, it is advisable to break it down into stages, the feasibility study being the first stage. Funding can then be sought for each stage from appropriate bodies. For example, a commission can be broken down into feasibility study, design stage, community consultation and workshops, production of work, launch and, finally, the documentation of the project as a whole in the form of brochure or video.

Why a strategy?

This chapter has illustrated that a strategic approach to fundraising is based on common sense and dealing with real situations. Visual artists should be good at it because, like making art, it is all about assessing situations and coming up with creative solutions.

Follow-through

Equally as important as gaining funds to undertake a project is the requirement to fulfil all the terms and conditions under which grants, goods or services were given.

- Conditions of grant aid, as defined in an offer letter, must be followed or you stand the risk of having to give back a grant. Conditions may include writing a report within a specific time-scale and providing a financial statement of how the money was spent or receipts to verify that a grant was spent correctly.
- Verbal agreements should be followed up in writing to avoid misunderstandings.
- Conditions of sponsorship – ie how a sponsor is acknowledged – should be agreed in writing, including whether publicity and other material about the project has to have their approval.
- If a project has several funders and sponsors, confirm use of logos and the order in which funders will be listed. Make sure all names are included on each item of publicity.
- Sponsors and funders should be invited to come to the exhibitions, events or unveiling of works they have assisted. This is not only to prove they have taken place, but part of the process of nurturing their interest in the arts. These events provide an opportunity for you to deepen their knowledge of the visual arts by showing them your work, asking their opinion, and also by introducing them to other noteworthy people including artists and local critics.
- If funders are unable to come, make sure they are sent photographs of it, along with any catalogue or other printed material, copies of press cuttings and details of any media coverage. These should not be sent as a loose sheaf of papers and slides, but suitably collated and professionally presented in a folder or booklet with a personal covering letter.
- Keep funders informed not only about the project they are assisting but also about what you are doing next. For example, tell them the exhibition will be touring, another piece has been commissioned, you are doing a residency in another school, etc. This encourages them to develop their involvement in the visual arts, perhaps by sponsoring another visual arts project in the future.
- As part of your long-term strategy to create and maintain fruitful relationships, add the names of sponsors and funders to your mailing list for future activities.
- Keep an annotated list of the outcome of successful and unsuccessful fundraising applications to save you time in the future.

3 • Making proposals

Eddie Chambers and **Yvonne Deane** with additional material by Susan Jones & Helen Smith

Whether applying for an advertised opportunity or initiating your own project, you need to know what factors make an interesting, attractive and coherent proposal, and to understand what the people and organisations who control and shape opportunities are looking for. The key to getting your ideas realised lies in your ability to put over yourself, your work and your ideas in person and on paper.

Previous art practice should be viewed as a springboard for subsequent work which may be of a radically different nature. If you are practising as a printmaker, ceramicist or painter, you still have the potential, for example, to execute a public commission as successfully as artists who have already had extensive experience of working in non-gallery environments. Your previous work may be just what makes you an attractive consideration. Documentation of past work indicates much more than just what you do. It shows your working methodology, the ways you critically interpret or engage ideas, your aesthetics, your sensibilities and so on. These considerations are often used to assess an artist's or maker's work, rather than just looking at how good a 'painter', or 'ceramicist' he or she may be.

To summarise, those in a position to give work to artists are more often than not concerned with how and with what consistency you have approached previous work, and are looking for clues to how you might approach a fresh project.

Approaches

There are, however, differences between the approach needed when artists apply for advertised opportunities, and when they seek to generate support and interest in their own propositions and ideas. A suitable word to characterise this is 'empowerment'. One approach has a greater degree of control, autonomy and empowerment than the other.

If you apply for a widely advertised opportunity, without doubt you'll be one of several hundred artists applying. Good slides, a clear covering letter and a carefully constructed CV should give you a decisive edge over other professional artists applying. Even so, most of the ideas and concerns informing the project brief will be essentially of someone else's construction. The best you can hope for is that someone will take a particular interest in your submission.

Even if you secure some interest, you still need to go a considerable distance to convince the project's organisers you are a suitable candidate. This may involve interviews or submitting more detailed information. At all stages, the power to 'select' or 'develop' your proposal lies firmly with people other than you. You can hardly be said to be 'making your own way'.

But if you choose to construct the terms of reference and creative parameters of a project wholly conceived and initiated by yourself, the process of personal empowerment becomes all too obvious. You may not ultimately succeed in executing your idea, but at all times you will have been in a more dignified and empowered position – one of unilaterally developing and seeking to execute your own ideas about art. Because you can develop ideas more closely aligned to your personal position and situation, it can be argued that they stand a significant chance of realisation. A self-initiated project also allows you the vitally important possibility of developing a work that is consistent with your own political or social sensibilities and agendas.

There are drawbacks to do-it-yourself projects, not least of which is the amount of time spent on administration. But as a comparison, it is estimated that only 5% of an architect's time in any project is involved with the creative and imaginative work. Some artists may find this a heavy burden, although others recognised it as part of the job, and time spent on administrative work is offset by the advantages of being able to develop a project in the way that best suits their work.

Some benefits:

- exercising control over your own project
- ensuring your work gets public exposure
- the chance to create challenging work on your own terms
- collaborating with people of your own choosing
- working with related professionals like architects, designers, curators, engineers, educationalists, etc
- building on strengths, interests and expertise
- expanding and improving technical and administrative skills
- expanding artistic possibilities in terms of scale or materials

Kinesis

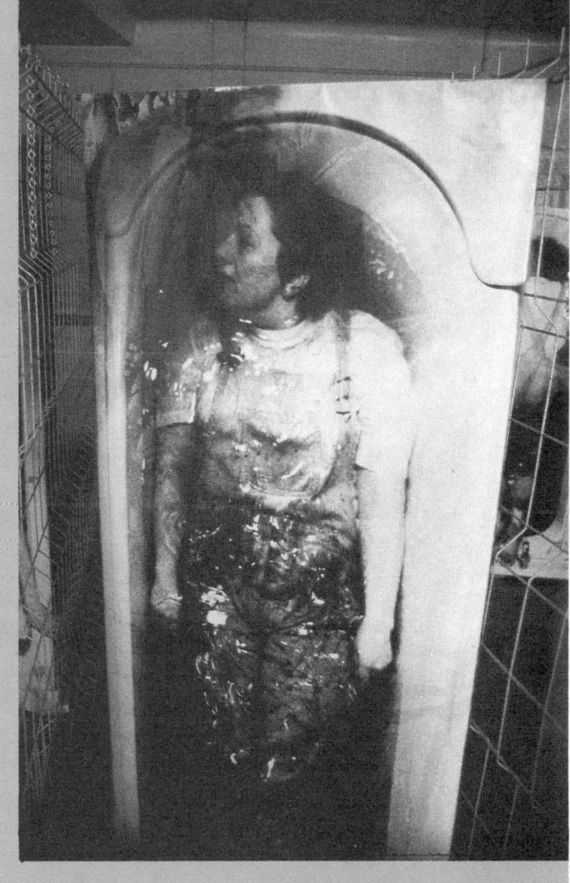

Detail from *Waste,* an installation by Susannah Silver **in the bathroom of the Old Model Lodging House, Aberdeen. Photo:** the artist

"In the bathroom, we inspect others. How does it feel to be them? We stand separated by the thin line of there-but-for the-grace-of-God."

Following a six-month residency in 1991 in Niort, Western France funded by Eurocreation where she was able to work on proposals to the city council for large-scale works concerned with art, architecture and environment, Susannah Silver returned to London but found it difficult to settle again. An invitation to do three days teaching at Gray's School of Art, Aberdeen led to the offer of a teaching post and development in August 1992 of Kinesis Artists Group – Susannah Silver, Susan Glasgow and Allan Watson.

Their initial idea was to convert The Old Model Lodging House (a former doss house) into temporary studios and hold an exhibition of site-specific installations by Kinesis and invited artists before the building was demolished and rebuilt as flats for single homeless people. Their proposal was supported initially by Aberdeen City Council who offered a grant of £1300 providing they showed that other donations had been received. Each artist donated £30 to release this grant whilst a fundraising campaign was activated to local companies. This meant that although the grant was offered in October 1992, it was not received until January the following year.

During the remaining six-months planning period, the group realised it was not feasible in the time to establish studios and mount an exhibition. It would have been costly to install power and secure the building, and no money would subsequently have been left for the exhibition.

When these difficulties were explained to the city council, they were agreeable for their funds to be used solely for an exhibition. The modified proposal was greeted with interest by the Scottish Arts Council who offered a guarantee against loss of £1500.

Shown from 18 April to 2 May 1993, the exhibition, which included work by invited artists Martyn Lucas and Annette Robinson, was also assisted by Aberdeen District Council, Langstane Housing Association, Greenham Janitorial Ltd, Anderson's Packaging Ltd, Conoco UK Ltd and Grampian Regional Council. John Lewis Partnership, Keith Johnson & Pelling Ltd, James Mutch Ltd, Travelstock Packaging, National Westminster Bank (Aberdeen) and Langstane Press supplied free goods or services. Discounts on materials came from SGB Scaffolding, Woolworth (Aberdeen), Phototechnical Services and Edinburgh Tile Distributors.

"The important thing is not to be self-conscious about doing a project like this. We weren't choosing a wacky place in which to put an exhibition because it would attract funding. Rather, we had found a location which was right for us. We arrived at an idea which was soundly linked with the development of our work."

An opportunity for Kinesis to exhibit in France came about through this project, and resulted in an installation in a disused bath-house as part of Niort's 1993 festival of public art for young artists of all disciplines. Susannah Silver was also invited to propose an installation for the town's main water tower, working to a budget of £130,000.

- getting funds to make new work
- developing work opportunities.

Some disadvantages:

- having to operate like a 'small business', dealing with planning, financial control, time-management, public relations
- time spent preparing proposals with no guarantee of success
- time and cost of doing your own negotiation, project management and administration
- doing your own problem-solving if anything goes wrong.

Making a proposal

Making a proposal is the opportunity to capture the imagination and interest of future partners or funders. It needs to anticipate and answer all the questions which the receiver is likely to ask about the project. It should cover the headings and points listed below. This is not only for the benefit of the recipient, but also to ensure the artist has thought the project through, and is confident it is feasible and practicable.

Who, when, where

- Details of artist(s)
- Anticipated date
- Who else will be involved
- Venue or location
- Summary of project idea.

Aims

- Why you want to carry out the project
- Who the audience is
- What the benefits will be to you, audience, community, others who will be involved
- How the project relates to your other work
- What the outcome of the project will be – exhibition, environmental artwork, participatory event, etc.

Concept

- Design ideas or other visual material about a project or an artwork, including medium, size, subject

In the bag or in the bin?

To : Managing Director

Safebury's Superstore
Lea Barton

Dear Sir or Madam

I am an Artist and I've just left St. Michael's with a BA Honours Two Two in Art and Three Dimensional Design.

Artists Statement

My work is concerned with exploring the ephemeral qualities of consumer constructs in the late twentieth century through site-specific time-based installation work. I am seeking to expose the true meaning of sites in the context of today's media laden society giving rise to contradiction and paradox within mythical space.

I think that supermarkets have a responsibility to help Artists although not enough do. You could support an Artist by helping me with a project I want to do in your carpark. What I want to do with a group of other Artists is create a time-based piece called 'Decaying Packaged Culture II' which will embody the collision between Nature and Consumer Culture.

An old car will be sited outside the superstore,

filled with layers of fruits and vegetables like the strata in the earth's soil. It will be filled to the brim and then sealed with plastic cling film and labelled with a price which states 'The Earth'. As the riot of the car combines with a decaying vegetation we will photograph the piece at the same time each day and run workshops and talk to the Public to get their views on Consumer Culture. I think it will get a lot of publicity and attract people to the Superstore.

We need these things to realise this important statement:

20 packets cling film
Fruit and vegetables to fill the car - about
20lbs each of carrots, cauliflowers, strawberries, lemons, mushrooms, cabbages, tomatoes, apples and anything else you can spare.
10 rolls slide film.

Budget
Car (from wreckers yard) £72
Delivery £17
Administration £45
Materials £48·93
Artists fees £376

TOTAL £568·93

Yours Sincerely

A. Smith (BA Hons).

This example of a fundraising letter illustrates some of the most common ways of ensuring your proposal goes straight in the bin. It would be rare to find such a complete catalogue of errors in the same proposal. But remember, just one may seriously damage your chances, and several can be the direct route to rejection.

Comments

- ☒ Presentation: zero points. You come over as thoroughly unprofessional.
- ☒ Hand-written letters on coloured paper (which doesn't photocopy), glass-mounted slides with inadequate labels, unrelated press cuttings and long unselective CVs must be avoided. Present information clearly and only include what is relevant.
- ☒ Get the name and correct title of the person you are writing to; use the full address.
- ☒ Get to the point! A rambling letter which fails to state clearly what you are asking for in the first paragraph will irritate the recipient.
- ☒ What are the benefits to the sponsoring organisation? Tell them how this proposal will meet their objectives, enhance their image, gain positive publicity for them.
- ☒ Avoid art jargon. An incoherent artist's statement is not appropriate for a proposal. Details of your degree course and marks belong on a CV.
- ☒ Putting 'BA Hons' after your name and talking about 'Artists' sounds arrogant.
- ☒ Do your research. This company has a good record of supporting arts organisations and educational projects. Find out about it and get their guidelines. Flatter them by acknowledging their arts programme rather than antagonise them with your ignorance.
- ☒ Check the budget. This one is vague and the sums don't add up.
- ☒ Who is involved? Make clear how many artists are working together on the project.
- ☒ No time-scale. State when your project is planned to happen and how long it would last. You have omitted to state when the car would be removed.

☒ Pay attention to issues of public health and safety. A rusting car full of rotten vegetables in a public car park constitutes a health hazard.

☒ Don't whinge! Telling a company it ought to help artists is patronising and unlikely to enlist their support.

Store manager's comments

What a nightmare. A sheaf of photocopies, badly typed CVs and broken glass fell out of the envelope. When I finally found the letter I was horrified at what was proposed. I've stepped up security patrols in the car park and am thinking of alerting the police. Do these people think we are stupid? Buried in the art school waffle was a clear message, 'We despise supermarkets and packaged food and want you to pay us to create a ghastly mess outside your store'. I'm pleased to say we won't be supporting this group.

Safebury's has an excellent reputation in supporting high-quality art and education work through a national awards scheme. We also have a deep commitment to environmental concerns, have reduced packaging on our goods, encourage customers to recycle carrier bags and provide bottle bins in the car park. I have a small budget to encourage local arts and environmental projects.

We are currently supporting an artist in residence at Lea Barton Primary School. Zena Davies' approach couldn't have been more different. She wrote to me with the idea of recreating with schoolchildren part of the market garden that existed on the Superstore site in mediaeval times. The project wasn't completely worked out but it already had the backing of the headmistress.

Zena's proposal caught my imagination. We arranged a meeting and worked out all the details. The project does involve using the car park, which is always a worry in terms of public safety but both my Public Relations Manager and I were won over by Zena. She had a clear idea of what she wanted to do and convinced me she had the energy, enthusiasm and expertise to carry it out successfully.

The Market Garden project is attractive, interesting and educational and will enhance the image of the Superstore as a provider of fresh fruit and vegetables to the city over many centuries. That's the sort of reputation I want to project. We want to link into the local community through our support of artists, not alienate people.

- Visual documentation of previous related work, although this may be achieved by referring to previous work as examples.

Practicalities

- Outline of how the project will be carried out and the time-scale involved.
- Reasonably accurate breakdown of costs and possible sources of income if known.
- How people who will be affected by the project will be consulted and involved
- Supporting statements from people who will be involved.

Resources

- Workshop space or other space needed
- Any planning or other permissions needed
- Water and electrical services and access requirements
- Materials and equipment needed
- Transport requirements
- Insurance – personal, equipment and public liability
- Description of relevant health and safety requirements
- Time-scale for acquiring or ordering resources.

Curriculum vitae

A CV is an important tool. Not just a chronological list of education and qualifications, it should give a rounded picture of you as an interesting and unique individual, suited and well-qualified to undertake a project. A CV should be:

- up-to-date
- adjusted to fit the project you are proposing
- descriptive rather than a simple list
- typed and well-presented.

The brief

The term 'brief' describes a set of instructions and definitions which all parties to a project use as a guide to their responsibilities during its course. It differs from a contract because it is more descriptive, provides contextual information about, for instance, the history of a site, aims or needs of a host organisation or specific technical requirements for an artwork. It may be referred to in the contract and become part of the legal agreement with the commissioner.

The brief provides you, the client and anyone else involved with a constant point of reference. If necessary, it also provides the material to deal with legal disputes. It is therefore important to get the brief right.

Creating your own brief

For artists' own initiatives the basis of a brief is your proposal. In effect, you are suggesting that through discussion, you mutually develop your proposal into a workable brief for a project. As discussions progress, the project concept will inevitably change from your initial outline.

Such development is a natural part of the process of getting a project off the ground and the detailed brief evolves through a process of discussion, negotiation, amendment and agreement covering every aspect of the project. It is vital that all parties involved are in accord with a final brief which needs to contain details of:

- what the artist(s) will do – make a piece of work, hold an exhibition, undertake a residency, etc
- who they will be working with
- purpose of the project
- if making an artwork, the location or suggested site – usage, cultural and social factors, etc
- if a residency or exhibition, information about venue and its users
- and for each stage of project's development including fees to artist(s)
- time-scale and deadlines
- administrative support, advisory groups and liaison points
- resources – studio, accommodation, equipment, etc and who will provide them
- any constraints on content, types of material, use of facilities, etc
- details of relevant health and safety requirements and provision.

Early research

In terms of creating an outline brief, there is no substitute for doing research at an early stage. The more work done identifying and costing materials, checking technical information and working out detailed time-scales and budgets, the more confident you will be about the proposal. This is particularly important for artists who regularly initiate their own projects.

Through research, you will find the companies who may sponsor your project, potential collaborators, local authority departments who can provide funding or support, and so on, and subsequently be able to pinpoint appropriate individuals to contact. The idea of finding and nurturing prospective and sympathetic 'allies' who can assist you now and in the future becomes of central importance. These are people who come to know your work and your aspirations well enough to commit funds or resources to it, and who may even be able to use their influence and commitment to your work to help generate more opportunities for you.

Equally important is the need to maintain and develop these contacts for long-term benefits. For example, local authority arts officers in the early stages of their career who become interested and involved in your work can grow into valuable supporters once they are in more senior positions and able to influence policies and budget allocation.

Follow-up

Personal contacts are a definite advantage when you come to follow-up speculative submissions to arts organisations. Once a proposal has been made, it is reasonable to telephone the person to whom it was sent and check whether it contains all the information they require, whether they foresee any difficulties with it, and when it is likely to be discussed. This should be done within seven to fourteen days of sending it, and the covering letter should say you will do this.

If you know it will be taken to a particular meeting, it is also reasonable to telephone the following day for an informal response. It may be that you will be asked for additional information for another meeting which will make a final decision, in which case the sooner you know that, the more likely you will be to be able to prepare it in time.

Be aware, however, that some organisations may be unwilling or unable to give information over the telephone. For example, the Foundation for Sport and the Arts states in their literature, "Our staff are not authorised to suggest timings, nor to speculate on the potential outcome of any particular case. When they say they are unable to give an answer it is because they are instructed not to do so, but also it is because they really do not know and can only mislead anyone who presses them into comment."

My Little World

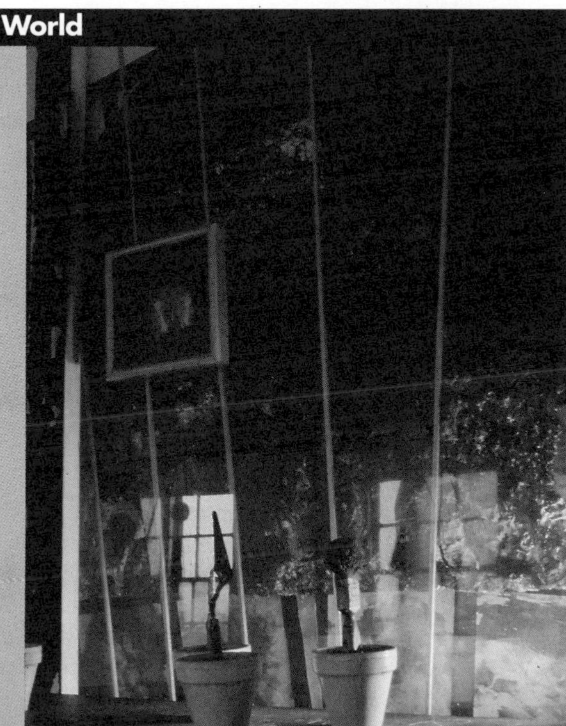

Robert D Clark, **detail of *My Little World – part seven*, 1993, mixed media.**

Robert Clark was one of 23 artists to receive a Yorkshire and Humberside Arts Board Artists Award in 1993. Sending a folder of slides, A4 sheet of information and applying for a 50% contribution to £3000 costs of developing his multi-media installation *My Little World* for exhibition, he was awarded £1000. The work will be shown in Leeds in 1993/94.

Each of the twelve pieces has developed from a base of 16' x 4' black cotton canvas pinned directly to the wall and is a complex assemblage of drawing, painting, poetic text, sculptural relief, re-worked books, sound devices and found objects and is a "kind of window in the form of a visual urban nocturne informed by references to memories of personal experiences, perceptions of places and work by significant historical artists and writers."

Presentation

No matter how strong or attractive an idea might be or how confident a visual artist is that with the right resources they can successfully execute the idea, presentation may ultimately be the pivotal and decisive factor in a proposal's success or failure.

Whether making a speculative proposal or an application, the same principles apply. Keep the paperwork 'short and sweet', thinking about how it will come over to the people who look at it. Not everyone who reads it will be an expert in contemporary art and its unique terminology, so avoid or explain artworld jargon.

Considering how the information will be interpreted by whoever will read it enables you to tailor the description of your work and your working methods to the best advantage. Put yourself in their shoes. What would you want to know? What would make the proposal come to life?

Quality control

Don't assume the originality and relevance of the creative aspects of your work carry most weight. There are other key factors which affect how a proposal will be received. The care and thought put into written and supporting materials will give the people reading it confidence in your professionalism and organisational abilities.

Bear in mind a proposal is likely to be photocopied, and because they will need to be handled throughout the selection processes, designs, artwork and slides need to be protected from finger prints and accidental damage.

Submissions should be typed, or at least legibly hand-written, concise, interesting and without art jargon, attractive but not over-designed, able to be photocopied – ideally no larger than A3 and produced in black or dark blue ink. They should be easy to handle, in a self-contained plastic folder for example.

Visual material

Good visual documentation of previous work, primarily in 35mm slide form, is the starting point for all successfully negotiated projects. It therefore follows that visuals included with a proposal must accurately represent your work and show it in the best possible light. Slides or photographs, labelled with your name, title, date and medium, should be in focus, correctly lit and show nothing other than your work. They should be suitably packaged to go through the post and easy to view – an A4 plastic slide holder is best. Don't send slides of work which isn't relevant to the proposal.

Many artists now also produce proposals in the form of a photocopied and bound document with a stiff or acetate cover, producing text on a typewriter or computer laser printer. Colour photographs or photocopies blown up from slides of previous work and linked to colour sketches or visual descriptions for a proposed new project can be bound in to make a cohesive document. Several copies can be made of a proposal in this way. An advantage is that material can be handled without fear of damage to original artwork.

There are also instances of artists producing their proposals in video format, this being particularly relevant for time-based or live work. Clips of previous work, linked with text or sound-track, can be used to present their ideas.

Portfolio

When putting together a portfolio to explain your proposal, consider how its contents are going to be presented and displayed to those making the selection.

A few good-quality and relevant pieces are preferable to a large quantity of previous works. A portfolio should be easy to flick through, with all items labelled. Provide a descriptive list of what it contains, just in case anything goes astray.

Proposal checklist

The contents of a proposal should include:

- covering letter on one side of an A4 sheet with summary of your proposal
- list of contents including designs or visuals enclosed with titles, medium, sizes, dates
- description of artistic concept with designs or visual material
- brief statement about your work
- up-to-date CV adjusted to the particular circumstances of the proposal
- if available, extracts from good press coverage of previous work
- pertinent extracts of descriptions of previous projects
- publicity brochure if available.

Put your name on each page and all the individual items, number pages and keep copies of everything including visuals. Don't send originals unless specifically requested, and if you do, try to insure them against loss or damage.

Personal presentations

The offer to give a presentation provides artists with the opportunity to keep control of their proposal, to emphasise and illustrate strengths and convince people that their idea is worth developing.

It shouldn't be too difficult to anticipate the types of questions that may be asked, but it is also not unreasonable to seek advice from other artists if you are unsure of how to handle it.

When making a presentation, make as much generalised eye contact as possible with the people to whom you are explaining your idea. Take along a copy of your proposal so you can refer to key points in it as necessary. Take time before answering complicated or difficult questions, but a few seconds should never be allowed to become awkward and extended silences. If you feel very nervous or make a mistake, feel free to take a deep breath, or ask for a glass of water.

Presentations are essentially a two-way process: your chance to get a response to your proposal, as well as the opportunity for others to ask detailed questions and gain assurance you are capable of undertaking the project.

Get it in writing

Once you have gained agreement that a project will go ahead, the most effective way of sealing that is to draw up a contract, a legally binding document which protects your interests. This can be done in a simple letter format, concisely referring to each of the points in the brief. In some cases, a more formal contract may be advisable. *An Introduction to Contracts,* published by AN Publications, outlines the context for contracts with basic dos and don'ts, and other specialist contracts cover exhibiting, selling, commissions and residencies are being published.

If no one else suggests putting a brief or agreement in writing, you must take responsibility for doing it and also for keeping your own notes of any discussions about the project. Never assume that someone else is working for your best interests!

Feedback may be hard to get but it is always worth asking for. Otherwise, how else will you know why your idea wasn't accepted, or indeed why you got it? Feedback, however painful the idea of rejection, helps you learn from experience and adjust your approach next time.

Be aware, however, that organisations will not always give an explanation. Although phrases such as "We received many excellent proposals and unfortunately we were unable to support all of them" may be true, they are also likely to be used to respond to those applications which were immediately rejected as well as those which were looked at more carefully.

Working successfully in the visual arts involves artists in developing confidence in their own potential and the ability to assert themselves as professional partners with others, whilst at the same time retaining the integrity of their ideas. Doing your own retrospective assessment of an application or proposal is therefore an integral part of that development.

Reviewing previous proposals

Working speculatively involves artists in investing time and money to submitting proposals, many of which will not succeed. However, although a proposal may not have been taken by one organisation, providing you are sure the idea is sound, you can turn a rejection to your advantage. For example, a proposal for a school project may not have been taken up by your chosen venue, but another may be interested once the idea is reviewed and appropriately amended to fit their particular interests.

There are other ways of using material. For instance, documentation from unrealised proposals including models or maquettes may be included in gallery exhibitions to help interpret an artist's thought processes as well as illustrating future projects to potential clients or sponsors.

Publicity

Although documenting a project is often a requirement of public funding, do not assume this is the only reason to do it, as it can equally be used to influence prospective sponsors, funders, commissioners, purchasers and collaborators.

For example, visual and textual material from a number of related projects can be edited and condensed into a brochure aimed specifically at people who have expressed interest in your work. Such a brochure could be composed of colour images laser-copied from slides, sections of text taken from a longer document and copies of cuttings from press or media comment. Favourable comments from noteworthy people may also be incorporated, and these can be altered according to circumstances. For instance, an enthusiastic comment from an art critic is appropriate in a brochure to a gallery whereas a

Environmental project

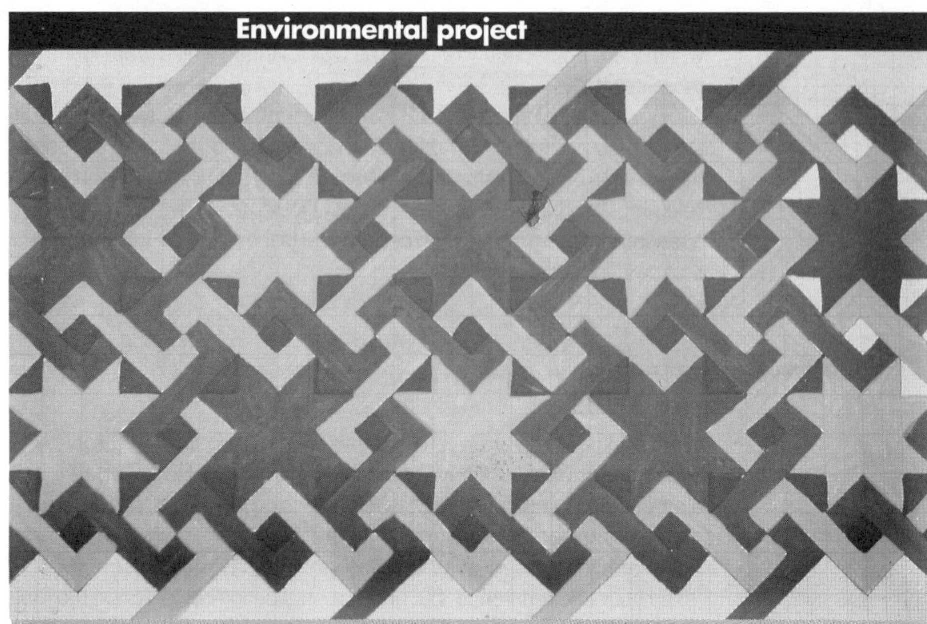

Lotus design by Anu Patel **for Norton Hall. Photo:** the artist

Anu Patel was invited in the summer of 1993 to work with city architects to produce designs for decorative paving, as part of the first phase of a scheme to re-landscape the area surrounding Norton Hall, a community centre in Saltley, Birmingham used predominantly by Muslim women and children. A collaboration between Birmingham City Council through the Museums & Art Gallery, Norton Hall and the South Asian Visual Arts Festival, costs of the commission are integrated into the landscaping scheme which is financed by inner city partnership funds. Additional funds are being sought to commission further works for a second phase of the scheme.

business sponsor is more likely to be impressed if the recommendation comes from someone else in the business world.

The financial report required from groups by funding bodies can also be turned into a publicity item. The Cardiff-based Pioneers, who undertake art in public and residency projects in South Wales, use their illustrated annual report as a summary of achievements, circulating it to press and media as well as to funding bodies and clients.

Planned development

Most visual artists keep their options open, applying for interesting opportunities as they are advertised, ensuring slides and documentation are on indexes and registers and also preparing their own proposals at the same time. Each artist has to be clear about what is right for them. Being objective and recognising capabilities and limitations enables artists to plan and assess development of their work, and not become worn down by rejection.

A focused, agile and creative artist can make much headway with developing their own proposals, simply because he or she at all times maintains a critical degree of control. After all, an artist has much less to 'lose' if his or her speculative ideas bear little or no fruit. But if they succeed, and a situation of mutual respect is created between artist and commissioner, the gain in the long-term is enormous.

4 • The financial side

Simon Pallett

Almost any application for funding will require a budget to be submitted, although budgets shouldn't only be prepared for applications or proposals, as they are a valuable tool for planning the financial side of your work and monitoring how well you are doing.

A budget is a financial plan covering income and expenditure. It may be for one particular project or it may be for a period of time. As well as helping in planning and monitoring, budgets help you to work out realistic prices for your work, which you can amend annually to ensure you earn a reasonable living.

Project & period budgets

Although budgets can be for particular projects, for example a residency, or for a period of time, say a year, in reality you will probably need to use both sorts. An annual budget provides a planning framework within which budgets for specific projects – which may be linked to funding applications – can be drawn up.

Drawing up an annual budget in advance may seem problematic because you won't know in sufficient detail what projects you will be undertaking during the year, what funds will be raised and what opportunities will present themselves. Nevertheless a base budget for the year can and should be prepared, with details relating to specific projects added later as they become available. In particular, this base budget should identify those basic running costs which you will incur regardless of what level of artistic activity you undertake eg workshop rent, telephone rent and insurance. This will help you to identify those overheads which need to be recovered through sales of work, project income or income from related activities, although they do not themselves constitute part of the direct costs of such activity.

A project budget should concentrate on the additional costs you incur through undertaking the project and the income it will bring in. A description of how to build a share of your overheads into the costs of a project or product is contained later in this chapter.

Types of expenditure

Any project or product involves the following types of cost:

- materials
- labour
- expenses – often called overheads.

It is also quite legitimate to include something for profit. Commercial businesses do it all the time. Although you don't have outside investors to whom to pay a return, profits can supplement your income and provide funds needed for capital expenditure in the future. Reviewing each element of cost in turn helps to develop a systematic approach to budgcting.

Materials

How you deal with materials costs depends on whether:

- your materials are of high or low value
- your materials can be readily attributed to a particular project or product.

With regard to the question of value, if you sculpt in marble or make jewellery with precious stones and metals, careful planning of material costs will be essential. If you use scrap or low-value items, it isn't worth the administrative effort to cost materials accurately, and materials costs are best treated as overheads. This method is described later in the chapter.

Sometimes it will be easy to attribute materials costs to a particular project, as with the sculptor above; at other times it may be too much trouble. For instance, can a printmaker cost how much ink goes into each print? It almost certainly isn't worth the trouble, because it would be difficult to calculate exactly how much and the value of materials is relatively low.

It is therefore important to assess carefully which method of allocating materials costs is best for your work, so that they can be built into your budgets. Of course, it may be appropriate to deal with some materials in one way, and some the other. For example, a printmaker may attribute paper costs to a particular project as the paper is expensive, but will treat the costs of cleaning solvents as an overhead cost.

Other points to watch:

- Allow for wastage, as it is all the materials which go into the process which count, not only those used in a finished product. You may also need to consider where wastage occurs in your creative process: a potter doesn't waste clay at the throwing stages as any waste is recycled, but if a bowl cracks in firing, not only are the materials wasted, but also labour and other costs which went into its making.
- Keep records of material usage especially for larger items, as this helps you budget more accurately in future. Without the benefit of past records, it may be very difficult to estimate the amount of wood in a sideboard or paint for a 10 metre long mural.
- Don't spend lots of time calculating the cost of low-value items, but make sure you get the big ones right.
- Err on the side of plenty when estimating materials costs. It is better to over- rather than under-estimate them.

Labour

Taxable profit is calculated according to specific rules. It is an artist's total income, less expenditure incurred on materials and overheads relating to their business. What an artist pays themselves is part of that profit. Although many self-employed artists employ an accountant to advise them and negotiate their tax liability with the Inland Revenue, others do this themselves.

Labour is also often described as 'fees', and is probably the trickiest item in the budget, as it involves putting a value on your time. It is also usually the largest item, as it is essentially your time that you are selling. A systematic approach to costing labour involves the following stages:

- Calculate how many 'productive' hours' (or days', although hours are better) work you intend to undertake during the year. Productive means directly income-generating. There are many essential tasks which do not directly earn anything, eg tidying up, applying for funding, administration, training, marketing, etc. Also don't forget to allow for holidays, illness and time to recharge creative batteries. If you know you will be doing any other paid work, allow time for it as well. Past records of how you have used your time are valuable, and may also help you to improve time management and your earning capacity.
- Set yourself an annual earnings target. Don't undervalue yourself and set the figure too low. Don't forget that self-employed people pay tax and national insurance on earnings once taxable profit has been assessed by the Inland Revenue. Self-employed people also often take out personal pension schemes and these costs have to be taken into account when working out an annual earning target. It is worth talking to other artists about reasonable rates and checking against fees offered for advertised residencies and commissions and what regional arts boards and arts councils recommend as minimum rates. Remember, however, that you will only realise your target if you can achieve as many productive hours as you estimate and if expenditure is kept within your budget.

See also *Money Matters: the artist's financial guide* from AN Publications.

See AN Publications' *Fact Pack: Rates of Pay* for a summary of current rates for commissions, residencies, running workshops and other work undertaken by visual artists.

Calculation of hourly work rate

Cabinet maker Sutapa Patel works 40 hours a week, but estimates only 75% of her time is productive. She wants to allow four weeks a year for holidays and two for illness.

Productive hours per week	= 40 hours x 75%
	= 30 hours
Weeks worked per year	= 52 – 4 – 2
	= 46 weeks
Productive hours per year	= 30 hours x 46 weeks
	= 1,380 hours
As her gross income target is £12,000 per year, her hourly rate should be:	£12,000 divided by 1,380 hours, giving an hourly rate of £8.70.

Expenses (overheads)

These are general running costs incurred over time which cannot usually be attributed to a specific product or project. A systematic way is therefore needed to build them into project costs, otherwise you won't cover costs and will incur losses.

If, exceptionally, you have expenses that can be attributed to a particular project, they can be shown separately, eg equipment hire or insurance or fees paid for particular services provided for a project.

The first stages in dealing with overheads which don't relate to a particular project is to identify overhead expense categories. This is not as easy as it sounds, since it is all too easy to omit some. It is sometimes possible to include a proportion of some domestic bills, eg business telephone calls made from home, proportion of car running costs, costs of using space at home if you work there, etc. Keeping records helps you identify all overhead costs and judge their level in the future.

Capital items, for example purchase of equipment or a vehicle, should not be included in overheads. It is nevertheless legitimate to include in overheads an allowance for the wearing out of equipment – called depreciation – or a provision for equipment replacement, although very small value equipment purchases can be treated as overhead expenditure. Finally, don't forget to build into your budget some allowance for the cost of training courses as you may need to take one in, for instance, welding or marketing.

The next stage is to quantify overhead expenditure for the year. Most people use past information and adjust it for inflation. If you do this, bear in mind that inflation applies at different rates to different items. Don't just add, say, 5% to everything, but look at each budget item and

A comprehensive list of tax deductable expenses is contained in *Money Matters: the artist's financial guide*

decide what inflation rate is reasonable to apply. You must also consider changes in circumstances. Adding inflation to last year's figures assumes the coming year is going to be very similar, but if, for example, in the coming year you will personally invite potential purchasers to your exhibition previews, the budget allowance for postage and stationery will need to be increased by more than inflation.

Points to watch:

- Concentrate on getting the large items right and don't spend too much time on small ones.
- Don't try to be overly precise, but calculate figures to the nearest £10, or even £100 on larger projects.
- Include VAT in your figures where relevant, unless you are registered for VAT, in which case figures in your budget should exclude VAT.
- If you don't have past records to refer to, take advice from friends and colleagues in similar positions as their budgets may give you a better idea of what to put in your own.
- Some costs, for example rent or council tax, are set in advance and can be predicted accurately. Others, such as heating, are much more difficult and depend on circumstances outside your control.
- If in doubt, over- rather than under-estimate.
- Some expenses are more easily controllable than others. For instance, although you could stop expenditure on marketing once your budget figure is exhausted, you can't stop consuming electricity. Thus your electricity budget needs to be an estimate of likely costs, whereas the marketing budget will be what you are prepared to spend.
- Include an allowance for low-value materials which can't easily be attributed to a particular project.

Calculation of depreciation

Fred Smithson has bought a new printing press costing £5,000.
It should easily last five years.
The annual allowance for depreciation which he should build into his overhead budget is therefore £5,000 (cost) divided by 5 years (estimated life) = £1,000 per year.

Calculation of replacement provision

Jenny Bland inherited a kiln when she began her business as a potter.
It cost nothing, but as it is old she estimates in four years time she will need to replace it, at a cost of £2,000.
Therefore the annual provision for kiln replacement should be £2,000 (replacement cost) divided by 4 years (estimated time to replacement) = £500 per year.

Once an overheads budget for the year has been established, it needs to be converted to an hourly or daily rate by dividing the total by the number of productive hours work expected in the year.

Calculation of hourly overhead rate

Sutapa Patel's estimated overheads for the year are £5,250. She estimates her productive hours for the year at 1,380.
Therefore her hourly overhead charge should be £5,250 divided by 1,380 = £3.80.

Sometimes labour and overhead charges per hour are added together to get a composite rate. For example, when trades people charge by the hour, their charge-out rate covers overheads and labour and includes an element of profit.

Composite hourly charge-out rate

Sutapa Patel is asked to provide 40 hours of time to a project.
How much should she charge?

	£
Labour	8.70
Overheads	3.80
Hourly rate	£12.50

Therefore her charge for 40 hours should be 40 x £12.50
= £500.00

It is important to base overhead charges on a full year's overheads to smooth out periodic ups and downs of expenditure. It is also easier to build in a modest allowance for items like training courses, costs of which are small in the context of an annual budget.

Contingency

A contingency is an allowance in a budget to cover unforeseen expenditure or shortfalls in income. It should not be an allowance for poor financial control, but a sensible precaution against accidents, sudden and unexpected price increases or strokes of fate.

It is quite proper, indeed advisable, to include a contingency in a budget, but you should be prepared to justify its level, as funders have a regrettable tendency to strike that cost out when funds are tight. There is no general rule about how large a contingency should be; it is a matter of judgement. Its size should be determined by careful consideration of the elements of the budget where there is greatest risk and on advice from others.

As an alternative, you can include an element of hidden contingency in each budget heading. Although this is less likely to be struck out by funding bodies, it may also make all your costs looks slightly inflated. This method can also create difficulties when you use the budget as a control mechanism (see later in the chapter) since overspending is less likely to be spotted.

Artists often base a contingency on a percentage of a budget, although the percentage used will be different on a small budget than on a very large one. For example, a studio group may add 10% (£600) to an annual overheads budget of £6,000 to cover unlet studios and unexpected repairs, whereas an artist organising an exhibition costing £500 may add 20% (£100) to allow for any increase in transportation and insurance costs.

Profit

When costing a product for sale it is reasonable to include an element of 'profit', although incorporating this in a funding application might be unwise, as funding bodies might not regard it as legitimate. In such circumstances, you should ensure the annual earnings target used to calculate an hourly labour cost includes your target profit for the year.

Note, however, that the 'profit' referred to here is not taxable profit, but earnings made over and above your gross income target, which you intend to plough back into your business to provide funds for future development – what other small businesses would call 'capital'. This could be used, for example, to buy time to undertake research or visit other countries or to allow you to purchase additional or more up-to-date equipment.

Applications for funding

The budget presented with a fundraising application will be based upon your own annual budget, but tailored to a particular funding body's requirements in terms of style and format.

Stages involved in putting a budget together

- Quantify materials costs which can be specifically allocated to the project.

- Quantify expenses which can be directly attributed to it.
- Work out how many hours' (days') labour it will take and multiply this by the labour rate you have calculated.
- Add an allowance for overheads based upon the number of hours as above and your hourly overhead rate per hour, calculated as previously described.
- Include a contingency which you should be prepared to justify.
- On the income side, give details of other sources of income, indicating whether they are confirmed, as funders like to see evidence of funding from other sources. Make it clear how much you are asking for from the funder to whom you are applying.

Alternatively, you could include a hidden contingency within the budget as described previously.

- If you receive sponsorship in kind, include it in your budget at a sensible estimate of its value to you. For instance, if you are receiving £500 worth of free publicity leaflets from a printer, £500 should be included within the sponsorship total and also shown as publicity expenditure. In-kind support thus involves matching items of income and expenditure and if you omit the in-kind support, you understate the sponsorship element in your budget, leading funders to conclude you haven't raised enough income from other sources. In-kind support can take many forms – materials, premises, accounting or marketing advice, etc. If you would have otherwise had to pay for it, it is quite legitimate to include it.

Some funders may not be happy with the simple description of one overhead figure and you may need to explain how this has been calculated. If this is not acceptable and a detailed breakdown of overhead costs is required, this can easily be done.

Shortfall

See also 2 • A fundraising strategy

Your budget was built upon certain assumptions about funding. If your funding is lower, you will need to revise your expenditure plans. It should not inevitably be the payment for your labour which is cut back to balance the budget. If your budget was realistic in the first place, then a funding shortfall can only be accommodated by scaling down the project, dividing it into stages, cutting out part of it or delaying the project until all the funds are found. You must not fudge this and just hope that things will turn out all right at the end of the day.

Basic headings for a fundraising application

Expenditure:	Materials
	Expenses
	Labour (or fees)
	Overheads
	Contingency
	Total costs
Income:	Regional arts board
	Charitable trusts
	Sponsors
	Sales (of work)
	Fees (for services, talks, etc)
	Amount applied for from this funder
	Total income

Control mechanism

You can use your budget as a mechanism for controlling and monitoring income and expenditure by comparing actual results with the relevant budget and reviewing differences. Accountants call these differences 'variances'.

You can do this by periodically comparing actual results with the budget for the same period. This involves dividing the budget when you draw it up into suitable time periods or stages of work.

Alternatively, take your results to date, add an estimate of costs to complete and income still to come, to arrive at an estimate of the project's final expenditure and income. Compare your estimated final result with the budget for the project and calculate the variances.

In estimating costs to complete a project and income still to come, don't just assume these will simply follow your budget as these will need reviewing in the light of your experience to date. For example, if the price of materials is higher than budgeted for, causing you to overspend, further overspending will arise on future materials purchases.

A format for drawing up budget reports is:

Extract from Budget Report

Budget head	Actual to date	Estimated costs to completion £	Estimated final results £	Total project budget £	Variance
Materials					
Steel	4750	4750	9500	10000	+500
Concrete	2625	5250	7875	7500	-375
Other materials	489	1461	1950	2000	+50
Total	7864	11461	19325	19500	+175

Variances should be investigated with a view, wherever possible, to taking corrective action, although not all variances are a cause for concern. Favourable ones, for example spending less than budgeted or achieving more income than budgeted, mean you are performing better than your budget. With these, your main concern should be to check that they are genuine and not the result of mistakes or delays in receiving bills. Some variances are too small to worry about. However, large adverse variances – spending more than budget or achieving less income than budget – should be investigated. What is large is a matter for judgement, but it is not solely a question of percentages. Being 50% overspent on a small budget head is likely to be less of a problem than being 5% out on a very large one. The aim of this monitoring process is to take action to at least limit the damage and, if possible, get things back on course again. In extreme cases you may have to revise your plans, and, where necessary, re-negotiate with your funders.

For comparison of actual results and budget to be useful, it should be carried out regularly and promptly, as corrective action takes time to implement and for improvements to happen. If you keep records of income and expenditure as you go along you will be able to produce an overall financial report soon after a project is complete, not only to give to funders, but also to provide accurate information for planning and budgeting future projects.

Cash flow management

Planning and managing cash flow is vital, since running out of cash will at the very least be highly embarrassing and at worst may prove fatal. It is easy to neglect this area, but it is just as important as planning your income and expenditure for the project. When you draw up your budget you should also plan when your cash is expected in, as well as when it has to be spent, to allow, for example, for grants which are usually paid in arrears, guarantees against loss, or for customers who are slow to pay up or fees paid on completion.

The best way to achieve this is to produce a cash flow budget. If you can, use a computer spreadsheet package to make it easier, but it can also be done with pencil and paper.

The example on the right shows, taking June as an example, that the month is expected to begin with a £5000 overdraft [shown as (5000) opening balance]. During the month, £6000 should be received, £5000 of grant aid and £1000 from sales. Expected outflows are £4500, made up of £2000 for materials, £2000 in artists' fees and £500 in expenses. Thus the position at the bank is expected to improve by £1500 (net change = £6000 – £4500), leaving the month end balance at £3500 overdrawn. July therefore starts with a £3500 overdraft. This draft cash flow could be used as the basis for negotiating better arrangements, see later.

The aim of a cash flow budget is to plan what the bank balance will be at the end of each period, to ensure that, from a cash flow point of view, your budget is feasible.

Points to watch

- Allow for delay between receiving a bill and paying it, providing your suppliers allow you to do this.
- Unless all your sales are strictly cash, allow for customers taking time to pay their bills.
- Don't include depreciation – it isn't a cash flow – but do include payments made for equipment purchase.

Positive cash flow management

Cash flow planning can bring significant benefits as well as helping to ensure you stay in business. It may occasionally identify temporary cash surpluses which can be put on deposit to earn a little interest. It can also provide the basis for negotiating an overdraft facility to deal with temporary financial difficulties, and it is always better to negotiate an overdraft in advance as it will cost you less. Furthermore banks are quite entitled to bounce your cheques if you overdraw without permission.

It also provides a basis for negotiating stage-by-stage payments from funders. It is worthwhile being proactive in this area by including a cash flow budget with requested stage payments with your application.

Example of a cash flow plan

	April	May	June	July	August
Receipts (cash in)					
Grants	5000		5000		5000
Sponsorship				5000	
Sales			1000	500	
Total	5000		6000	5500	5000
Payments (cash out)					
Materials	1000	2000	2000		
Artists' fees	2000	2000	2000	2000	2000
Expenses	2000	1000	500	500	500
Total	5000	5000	4500	2500	2500
Opening balance	0	0	(5000)	(3500)	(500)
Net change	0	(5000)	1500	3000	2500
Closing balance	0	(5000)	(3500)	(500)	2000

Notes

- Figures in brackets represent negative figures, either cash outflows under the heading net change, or bank overdrafts for opening and closing balances.
- The net change represents receipts for the month less payments for the month. It will be positive if receipts are greater than payments and vice versa.
- The closing balance for the month is calculated as follows:

  opening balance + net change = closing balance
- The closing balance from one month is the opening balance of the next.
- The example shows monthly periods which is the common way of dealing with finances, although any other suitable period of time can be used.
- A real-life cash flow budget would necessarily have many more headings than the example.
- The example shows the project will suffer severe cash flow problems, although by the end of five months, cash flow is healthy.

A guarantee against loss and the stipulation that the city council grant would only be released if other funds were found caused difficulties for the Old Model Lodging House project. As all artists involved were on a low income, the maximum they could contribute to the project's cash flow was £30 each. Susannah Silver had to persuade National Westminster Bank to provide a free overdraft facility and free bank account so there were some funds available to finance production of the exhibition.

Guarantees against loss are best avoided if at all possible, as they delay the final grant instalment until after the project is over and accounts have been submitted. If you can't avoid one, argue it should be kept as small as possible because of the impact on your cash flow. When claiming a guarantee you don't necessarily need to wait until you have actually paid all your bills. Provided you can draw up a statement of accounts for the project with reasonable certainty the figures are accurate, you can make the claim. You need to know how much the outstanding bills will be, but don't need to have paid them.

If you need to make claims from a funder for agreed contributions for materials, fees or other costs, issue them with an invoice just like any other professional would, using headed paper with date, description of the goods and services you are providing and put in their value.

Improving your cash flow

The healthiness of your cash flow depends on how well you manage your credit control, stocks of materials and the use of credit offered to you by suppliers.

You should therefore take steps to ensure income is received as soon as possible without going so far as to upset important customers or funders.

This can be done by:

- making clear to customers what your payment terms are and if you offer credit and stating this on your invoice and in any contracts you make
- chasing up slow payers and sending reminders
- issuing your invoices when you provide goods or services, as delay in issuing them will delay your receipt of cash
- claiming guarantees against loss promptly
- being up front about your cash flow requirements when applying for funds, using your cash flow budget to demonstrate need.

If you can get credit (time to pay) on goods and services you receive, it makes sense to take it, since it is effectively a short-term interest-free loan. Don't abuse it though, as you may upset important suppliers whose goodwill you need and may be unable to get credit from them in the future.

If material stocks are of significant value, good management of them will improve cash flow. Stocks of materials tie up money, so stock levels should be kept as low as possible without jeopardising efficiency. Don't buy in greater quantities than you need to, unless the discount is enough to compensate for tying up your cash. Avoid getting materials delivered too soon and take special care to order materials so that they arrive when you need them, neither too early or too late. The general aim should be to minimise the time between taking delivery of materials and receiving cash from your customers for goods and services provided.

Advice & training

Good management of your finances is crucial if you are to succeed with putting your ideas and proposals forward to potential funders. If you are unsure of book-keeping and how to understand your financial situation, don't just go forth with hope and optimism, as help is available.

Regional arts boards usually provide advice and information to artists in some form – if not face-to-face advice from officers, then information sheets or subsidies for training courses. They can often also direct you to other sources of advice.

Banks can provide small business advice in return for opening an account with them. Several offer free guides on business planning or preparing cash flow budgets.

See *Money Matters: the artist's financial guide* for the implications of using an accountant and the questions you should ask them.

Accountants not only check your book-keeping and make sure you have claimed all allowances and expenses before the Inland Revenue assesses how much tax you should pay, but also offer financial advice based on their knowledge of your particular situation.

Regional training centres and other organisations offering training, including those offering short courses in business skills which are of value to visual artists and makers, are listed in **Contacts**.

See 9 • Contacts
See 8 • Further reading

Training and enterprise councils, co-operative development agencies and Department of Trade and Industry regional centres are amongst a number of agencies set up to offer advice and training to small businesses.

Budget examples

The following is an example of an annual budget for an artist-run organisation showing overall summary and a budget for one of the year's projects.

Annual budget

Expenditure	Annual budget	Budget 6 months	Actual 6 months	Variance 6 months	Notes
Co-ordinator's fees	15000	7500	6250	+1250	Late appointment
Telephone	1000	500	453	+47	
Stationery	120	60	75	-15	
Office	2000	1000	1000	0	
Insurance	200	100	102	-2	
Electricity	340	100	125	-25	
Publicity	500	300	165	+135	Late printing of leaflets
Co-ordinator's travel	500	250	325	-75	Meetings with sponsors
Management committee expenses	600	300	290	+10	
Projects	80000	30000	25125	+4875	See budget report for each project
Contingency	2000	1000	0	+1000	
Total	**102260**	**41110**	**33910**	**+7200**	
Income					
Regional Arts Board grant	38000	19000	19000	0	
Local authority grant	30000	15000	15000	0	
Charitable trust	10000	10000	11000	+1000	Extra grant secured
Sponsorship	25000	10000	7500	-2500	Delayed decision on funds
Total	**103000**	**54000**	**52500**	**-1500**	
Surplus/Deficit	**740**	**12890**	**18590**	**+5700**	

Residency budget

Expenditure	Budget	Actual	Variance	Notes
Fee 10 days @£100 a day	1000	1000	0	
Materials:				
Paint	75	65	+10	
Paper	60	50	+10	
Brushes	25	30	-5	
Display	250	275	-25	
Artist's travel	50	45	+5	
Publicity	50	35	+15	
Documentation	100	95	+5	
Totals	**1610**	**1595**	**+15**	
Income				
Regional Arts Board grant	1000	1000	0	
Parent teacher association	400	400	0	
Sponsorship	210	150	-60	
Totals	**1610**	**1550**	**-60**	
Surplus/Deficit	**0**	**-45**	**-45**	

5 • Sponsorship in kind

Susan Foster

Artweek, an annual visual arts festival based in Oxford and the surrounding county, began in 1983 as an open studios event, run by Oxford Artists' Group, an association of professional artists. By 1987, the programme had grown to include art in public places events and education projects and required professional administration for co-ordination and fundraising.

I started work as an arts administrator on Artweek '88, with funding for administration secured largely through local authorities, in particular from Oxfordshire County Council. This left the problem of funding the major publicity item, the *Artweek Guide*, other promotional material and the projects. We did not necessarily need cash, indeed our needs were all obvious candidates for sponsorship in kind.

Mixed blessings

Sponsorship in kind comes with its blessings and headaches, as we were soon to discover. Many companies are in a position to help substantially and would like to make use of the PR, but can't commit cash. The trick is to draw up a shopping list of 'things requiring funding' in such a way that potential sponsors can easily identify some way to help, making it less likely that they will get off the hook altogether.

As a result, you get what you need and the sponsor gets good exposure, all with no exchange of cash. That's the good side: the headache comes with the fine-tuning, exact matching of what you need with what the sponsor can give, and with your relationship with the sponsor. In terms of the relationship, the problem is that you are not straightforwardly buying a service or product, and aren't in a position to dictate quality, quantity, adherence to time-table, and so on.

Although all these things may run smoothly, achieving success can also require the negotiating skills of a UN international peace-keeping team. Pluses and minuses of sponsorship in kind are illustrated here through examples drawn from my experiences with Artweek over a four-year period.

Business as Usual

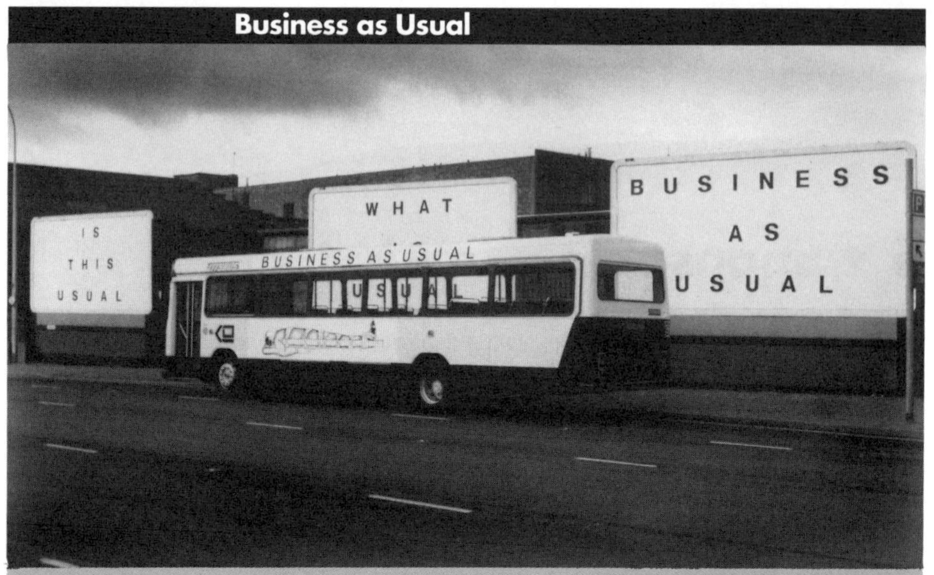

Colin Finley's public art project *Business as Usual* was created on three adjacent 20'x 10' billboards, with the statements 'BUSINESS AS USUAL', 'WHAT IS USUAL?' and 'IS THIS USUAL?' respectively.

'BUSINESS AS USUAL' is pasted over boarded-up shops in Belfast after a bomb blast to illustrate the shop-keeper's defiance of being put out of business, and the artwork questions for whom this is a normal occurrence. 'WHAT IS USUAL?' refers to the fact that 40% of Northern Ireland's population are under 24 (The 'Troubles' began in 1969) and don't know Northern Ireland without violence, terrorism and bigotry, and asks whether for the remaining 60% this is usual. 'It becomes too easy to accept what is happening here socio-politically as a form of normality. We become immune or numbed by the never-ending accounts of terrorism that a conscious effort has to be made to question – IS THIS USUAL?'

The artist made a personal approach to the Development Manager at Metro Advertising Group who liked the project and supplied a list of all their boards in Northern Ireland. Having picked which he wanted, the artist could make free use any of them – for this project or others – for one-week periods providing they were not booked by a commercial advertiser. Alexander Boyd Display hand-painted the boards for a nominal sum. The boards were sited on a main arterial route into Belfast at the end of the M2 in March, and the work was also shown outside Untitled Gallery Sheffield for the Media Show and in Denver, Colorado in April. To accompany the static work, Citybus loaned a bus on which a 15' image of a bandaged man taken from a 1st World War St John's Ambulance Brigade sling was pasted on each side and in large text above the windows it read 'WHAT IS USUAL?' and 'IS THIS USUAL?' on respective sides. Because of a series of attacks on bus drivers and passengers, however, rather than being on display around the city on the bus for a week, the work was created for photographing only. The cash value of sponsorship for billboard and bus project was estimated at around £1000.

Colin Finley often uses business sponsorship to enable his work, seeing it as an effective way to achieve work he otherwise couldn't afford to do. For his street signs project – a series of images manufactured to replicate actual Department of Transport signs with a socio-political twist which are planned to be affixed to posts around the city – a local firm willingly provided fabrication and printing, providing their name was not revealed. After a showing in Belfast in August, the work will be toured to London and Dublin as part of a group show from students on the MA in Fine Art at the University of Ulster.

Artweek guide

Having drawn up a shopping list, at the top was the *Artweek Guide* – the main publicity vehicle for the festival, containing maps with information about each Artweek site, details of opening times, photographs, editorial and sponsorship credits. If we had published it ourselves, it would have cost around £10,000.

One of the biggest local companies with in-house printing facilities was Oxford and County Newspapers. We wanted the up-market *Oxford Times* to produce one of their monthly glossies as the *Artweek Guide*, but were told this would be too expensive, might not be in line with the expectations of their posh North Oxford readership, and was out of the question. But how about the *Oxford Mail*, the daily local tabloid? The editor was keen, but it took a while at Artweek for the penny to drop that our guide would no longer be a handy, neat A5 booklet, but an unwieldy 12-page tabloid *Oxford Mail* supplement.

However, we decided to go for this. We needed to expand the festival, our major sponsor Oxfordshire County Council wanting to see a wider audience. What better way than through the *Oxford Mail's* 42,000 readership? Besides, we did not have an alternative sponsor, and time was pressing on. But how were we to get the Oxford Mail Artweek supplement into venues other than newsagents? We persuaded the newspaper to print free for us an extra 30,000 copies. The draw-back was that we could not take possession of them earlier than the selling day of the supplement – strategically set for one week before the Artweek opening. We therefore had to set up an efficient and fast distribution network for our copies. The newspaper's distribution team were brilliant in helping with this. They had the vans going out anyway and we made use of them, free of charge.

Next came the question of content. We felt there was relatively little room for negotiation, as the guide had to have a certain number of maps, minimum number of words per site and a little extra space for projects, photographs and minimum editorial. Furthermore, the editor was pleased we increased the number of participants by 30% on the previous year as the bigger the event, the more PR and exposure for the paper. This meant less space in the guide for editorial and more for listings.

We began to see the relevance of this when we submitted our editorial to the sub-editors. What we had not anticipated was that they would re-write it in '*Oxford Mail* speak'. Not the kind of image Artweek was aiming for. However, we negotiated our way satisfactorily through this and came to the next hurdle. How does a major sponsor allow another sponsor to be credited in a guide which, by now, was very much the property of the *Oxford Mail*? Hard-line but sensitive negotiations achieved a reasonable compromise.

Next came the question of design for the front page image, to be used also on all publicity material. Rather than ask newspaper staff to design it, we felt it better to get further sponsorship in kind by inviting the Head of Visual Arts at Oxford Polytechnic to design the poster and publicity image. This in itself was an exercise in tact. Having asked him to produce a free design for us, we were in no position to go backwards and forwards with rejections and suggestions for changes. Furthermore, the design had to suit the editorial staff on the *Oxford Mail* or we would find ourselves at their mercy with their own design. These issues were resolved and a satisfactory compromise found.

Finally, we submitted our proofed copy on disk, days in advance of the print deadline, and were subjected to the standard speedy newspaper time-table, being called in at a specific time to proof the entire text in an hour and asked to make as few changes as possible. (This was not the way we meticulously handled the proof-reading exercise in subsequent years.)

The guide went out and was fine. It reached thousands of new potential visitors – an important political bonus for us – and enabled us to divert the rest of the small funds to other projects. In broad terms working with the newspaper was a success, but we found ourselves constantly weighing advantages against disadvantages.

Art in public

That year we embarked on two new 'Art in Public Places' projects which contributed significantly to establishing Artweek as a major visual arts festival rather than an open studios event. The billboard and bus projects, only made possible through substantial sponsorship in kind, both developed through complex negotiations with sponsors.

Billboard project

What better way to place a large 'canvas' in a public space than to use a commercial billboard as a gallery? However, as we weren't in any position to buy the paper, let alone hire sites at commercial rates, we negotiated with Mills and Allen for a charity rate in exchange for credit in the *Artweek Guide*. Southern Arts paid the site hire at the reduced rate of £300 a week, and Mills and Allen threw in the paper. Although the paper quality was poor, the artists managed to use it successfully. However, because we were on the billboard company's charity rate, we could only select sites at short notice, provided they were not booked by

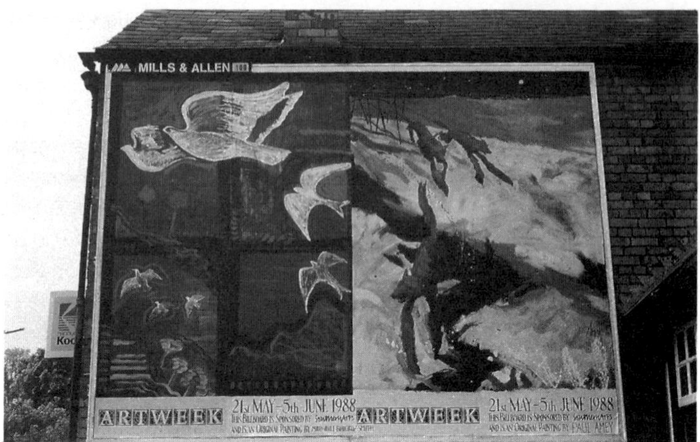

Images 8' x 7' by Malgorzata Bialokoz **and** Paul Amey **for the 1988 billboard project. Photo:** Artweek

commercial users. We selected ten boards around the city – some prime sites – and the paintings went up.

As far as public and media were concerned, this was an exciting pioneer project, attracting coverage on Radio 4's *Kaleidoscope* and a feature in *The Guardian* and other nationals. Exposure pleased Mills and Allen, but they were twitchy about dealing with artists, thinking they might produce sensitive and offensive images (never mind Benetton, Haagen Daz or many tobacco companies – they pay real money).

The next year we extended it to other Oxfordshire towns, selecting clustered sites in Oxford itself. We got the same charity rate for billboard hire, but by receiving sponsorship in kind, rather than paying the full hire fee, we didn't benefit from full contractual agreements, and experienced a lack of respect when sizes of some billboards were altered after artists had completed images, no care was taken with the work, and the Mills and Allen manager showed an almost threatening manner regarding censorship of images.

Worse was to come. The work went up for the agreed concessionary period of two weeks. However, Mills and Allen's left hand didn't know what its right was doing, and within a few days the majority of the 15 pieces were pasted over with commercial advertisements, the original paintings not even lasting the first week of the two-week festival.

These problems were frustrations behind the scenes. Despite that, we would certainly do it again, but would seek to raise cash sponsorship to pay full commercial rates for the sites and therefore be in a position to call the tune.

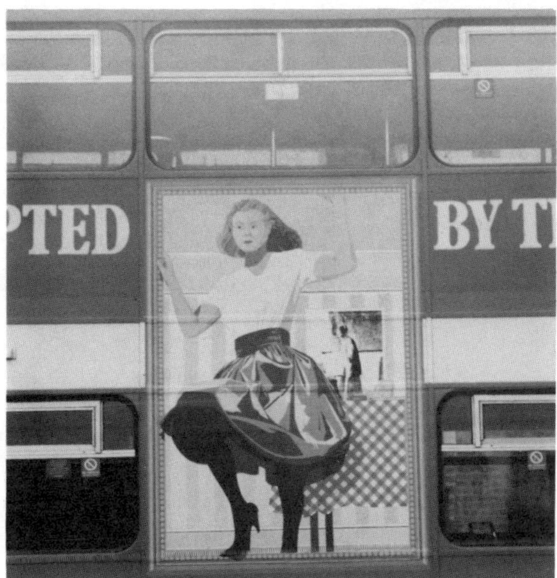

Original screenprint on vinyl by Brendan McGrath **on the side of an Oxford City Bus Company bus. Photo:** Artweek

Bus project

The bus project is an interesting example of sponsorship in kind because we succeeded in pairing up with three separate sponsors to make it work. We planned to use outside and inside advertising spaces on Oxford City Bus Company double-deckers. Both the bus company and the advertising agency agreed with no problem. From then on we dealt with grass roots workers, the traffics assistant and technician and they couldn't have been more helpful. For the outside of 20 buses we needed removable adhesive matt vinyl in large quantities as well as matt vinyl inks, fillers and screens. Vinyl came from Adhesive Display Products who supplied off-cuts, cut down to the right size. Inks, screens and fillers came from Sericol obtained through Oxford Printmakers' Co-operative who have a well-established relationship with the company. Ironically, although the project's theme was the Rain Forest, and Sericol were and still are developing a Green non-toxic water-based range of inks, inks available to us for the project were toxic oil-based ones.

We were given the use of advertising space inside over 100 double-decker buses, matching this with £500 sponsorship from Central Television one year and Southern Arts the next to pay for card cut to fit the spaces.

An added bonus from this relationship, was the bus company printing 5,000 handbills for display in all city and county buses – more publicity for the project than we could have afforded ourselves.

Materials sponsored

Tina Addison has made extensive use of in-kind sponsorship of materials in her work. "I didn't want my art work to suffer from having no money to buy materials, and I also wanted to be able to make work on a very large scale."

Whilst still a student at Staffordshire Polytechnic, she developed the technique of combining her paint with axle grease donated by Century Oils Ltd. She later went on to use 'obsessive amounts' of donated materials to create installations. For example, 50 kilos of peanut butter from Duerrs Ltd, 100 silicone teats from Cannon Babysafe, 50 kilos of strawberry blancmange from CPC (UK) Ltd, 600 toothbrushes from Addis Ltd, and 1000 donut centres from Dunkin' Donuts.

In April 1991, whilst an MA student at Glasgow School of Art, she undertook an exchange visit through DAAD (German Academic Exchange Programme) to Berlin. A Prince's Trust 'European Vision' award in 1992 gave her the chance to develop contacts there further. In 1993, an award of £400 from the Scottish Arts Council's Small Assistance scheme linked with acceptance of a place on the Kunstlerhaus Bethanien international studio programme enabled her to spend a year in Berlin. Installations there have also been assisted by donations of unusual materials. For example an installation in a circus tent in in Berlin utilised stale bread and cakes donated by a local firm.

Phaidon sponsorship

To obtain the next year's *Artweek Guide*, armed with impressive statistics on visitor numbers and our higher media profile, we approached Phaidon Press with a new shopping list. They agreed to publish it for us in-house – including design, typesetting, paste-up and printing – and to provide free office space for a year, giving us a street-level suite of offices in the city centre which could also be used as an exhibition space. The company also gave us 'old' office furniture to set us up.

Phaidon Press published the *Artweek Guide* for two years, giving us the chance in the second year to overcome some of the problems encountered in the first. Our main problem was that we were low priority with the design team. Because of this, the chief designer was prepared to spend only a very limited time on the guide. She produced a cover design which did not conform at all with the image we wanted to promote. Under pressure, she came up with a few alternatives and we selected the best but without conviction. Due to financial constraints, we were obliged to settle for a black and white rather than colour cover, and had to accept typesetting and layout as it came.

In contrast to the relationship with the *Oxford Mail*, Phaidon Press did not exercise any control over our copy. The following year we relieved pressure on the design team by paying for our own designer and providing final artwork ready to print. We also paid to get a full-colour cover. Phaidon still ran the entire print job for us, using their contacts with Robert Horne Company to obtain free (end of line) paper and cost-price printing. For two years running, we got 30,000 copies of a 56-page A5 publication valued at around £12,000 for next to nothing.

Painting Park

The Painting Park project also attracted an interesting range of sponsorship in kind, and followed on from the idea of the billboards. For a site for creating and siting a series of 12' x 8' paintings, we negotiated use of South Parks with Oxford City Council.

Although the City Council Arts and Recreation Department could not give us a grant to cover materials, we were able to help the Parks Department spend its surplus before the end of the financial year. The project was not run until May, but all materials were ordered in March, including 170 sheets of plywood, a hundred 12-foot-long 3"x3" posts, 2000 screws in specified sizes, three dozen household brushes, 32 litres of matt white emulsion and, importantly, two men with tractor and trailer to help erect and dismantle the structures.

The Parks Department also wanted to get some PR out of the project, and produced and distributed 5,000 leaflets using our design and artwork. This was a case where our requirements were exactly matched by materials, facilities and budget of the City Council Parks Department. On the strength of their support we also got the ninety 4' high metal Metposts needed to support wooden uprights for the painting area from Metposts Ltd at a fraction of cost price. When I first approached this Cardiff-based firm, I received a straightforward question: "Why? What's in it for us?" They decided to get involved, however, because we could offer exposure – the project attracted considerable media coverage – and because the event was being supported by other companies and agencies. It would have been far harder to raise funds to buy the posts at full retail price.

Zedcor gave us limitless industrial plastic sheeting, and, as we qualified for paint under the Dulux Community Projects Scheme, we carefully selected 300 litres of paint. However, our request came in at the tail end of the award and we seemed to receive a disproportionately

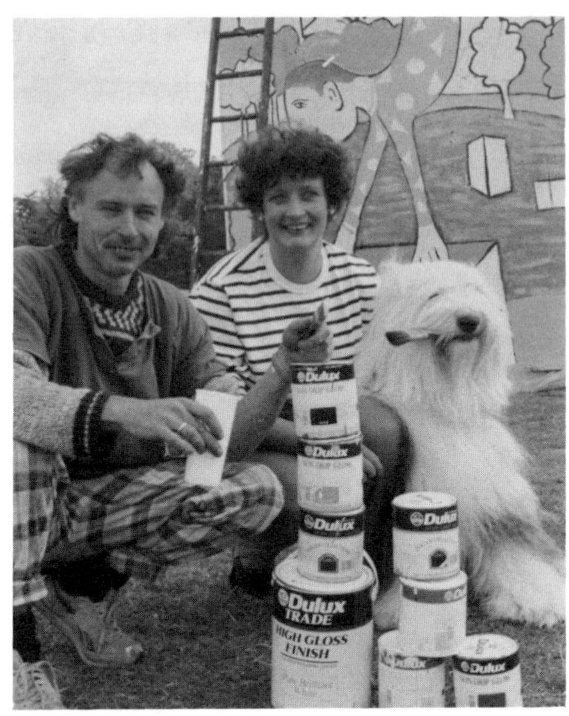

Rowan Vulgar, Alison Sellman from Dulux and Tanya the Dulux dog at the 1990 Painting Park. Photo: Oxford County Newspapers

large amount of magnolia coloured paint. Fortunately, a number of local paint companies also gave paint. Dulux was keen on our scheme, largely because of media attention and because it presented good photo opportunities for Tanya, the Dulux dog.

International Plener

An advantage of sponsorship in kind is that it can be used to lever cash funding. When Artweek organised the first International Artists' 'Plener' – a Polish word used to describe a short period when artists live and work together to develop work, make contact with other artists, and to engage in discussion and debate – the £16,000 project attracted £7500 from the Arts Council International Initiatives Fund and £3000 from their Research and Pilot Projects Fund, both conditional on a reasonable level of matching funding.

We were able to show matching funding by giving a monetary value to all sponsorship in kind. Paper from John Purcell Paper was valued at £200, exhibition costs from Oxford Exhibition Services – who

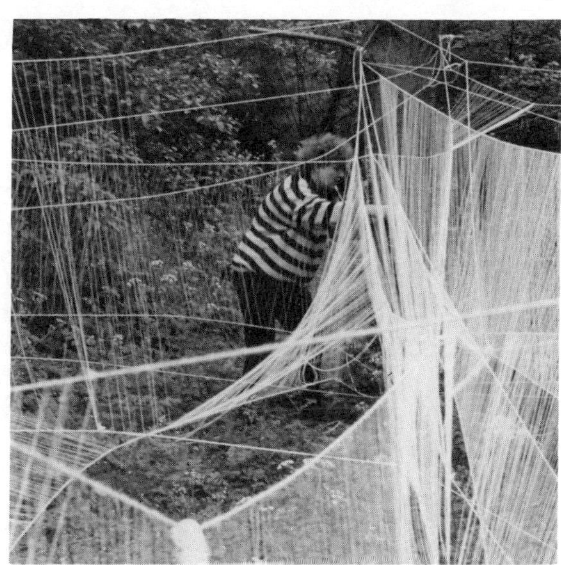

***Imaginary Roads* by** Bohuslava Olesová **made at Sutton Courtenay Abbey during the International Artists' Plener in 1992. Photo:** Artweek

lent frames, screens and van and gave technicians for hanging two exhibitions – at £500, and the artists' travel costs were paid by a number of sources including the British Council in Poland, Jagiellonian Trust, Bonn City Council and Jan Hus Education Foundation, estimated at £3500. All could be entered under 'expenditure' and 'income' headings in the budget to ensure release of Arts Council grants.

Close relationships

Sponsorship in kind is a valuable supplement to cash sponsorship and the same rules apply in terms of offering exposure and perks to sponsoring companies. With cash sponsorship, however, the artist or arts promoter offers to provide public exposure and publicity in exchange for the sponsor's cash. But with sponsorship in kind, the sponsor's products or services are swapped for publicity and public exposure. It is therefore more like a bartering system.

To gain in-kind sponsorship it is usually necessary to establish a close relationship with company staff, both at management level as well as further down the line, to get the balance right. Getting the relationship working well, however, will lead to the type of positive relationships which have been described here. In addition, awareness is raised within the business world of the value of working with visual artists. This may have the longer-term benefit of encouraging more businesses to sponsor artists' projects in future.

Charged Atmospheres

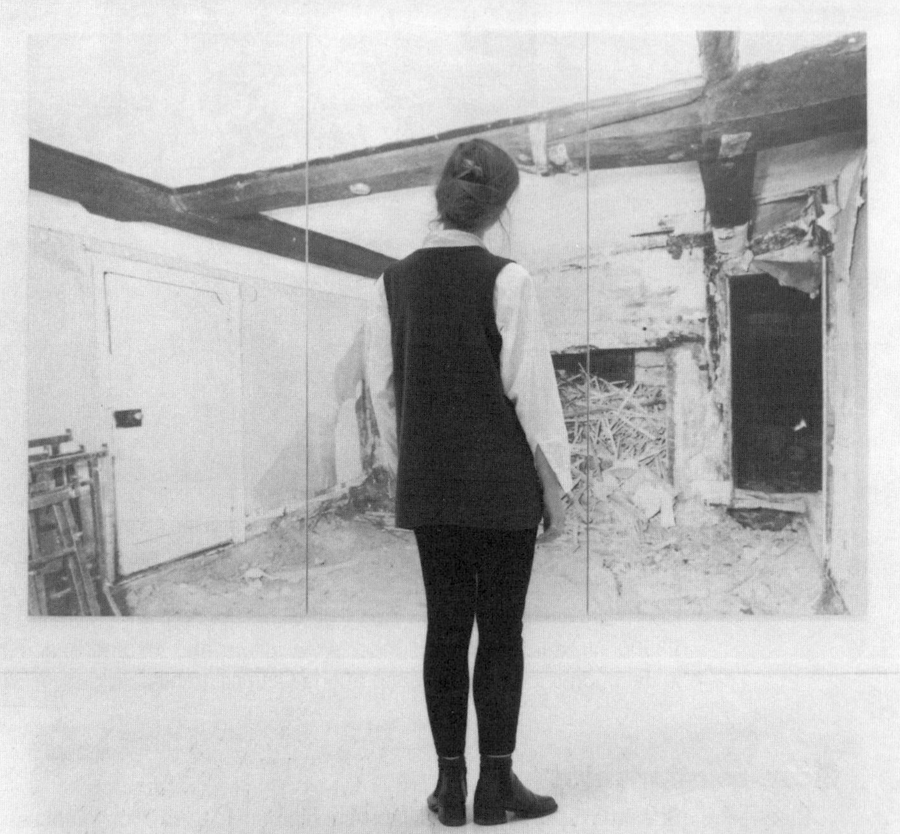

Alison Marchant's **installation** ***Charged Atmospheres*** **comprised a series of 8' x 10' photographic images based on dilapidated interiors of country cottages and stately homes of the 1970s. Commissioned by Camden Arts Centre, the exhibition was also shown at Southampton Art Gallery, Cambridge Darkroom and Old Museum Arts Centre Belfast. Photo:** FXP Photography

During the late '80s, Alison Marchant began making large-format photographic images which were sited on streets, in derelict buildings and in galleries. At 8' high, they were too big to be printed in an ordinary darkroom, so she used enlargement and mounting services of a local firm, Sky Photographics, whose work is predominantly for companies. Having built up a relationship with the staff over a period of time, a receptionist suggested she should apply for sponsorship. Soon after, an agreement was reached with Camden Arts Centre to show an exhibition of new work with the possibility of touring it. Funds had also been raised from the Arts Council, London Arts Board and Elephant Trust. A formal approach to Sky Photographic by Camden Arts Centre on the artist's behalf led to an offer to provide copy negatives, proof prints and 8' x 10' heat-sealed enlargements valued at a substantial amount. The company manager was not interested in the work's socio-political content, rather how the company would be credited, and where the exhibition would tour.

"It was not easy to get this assistance. It came out of a lot of work and patience and determination to see the project through. It is important to gain strength from looking and appearing positive in various situations – this is polite if nothing else. You must come across well to those who show an interest, not revealing your doubts or worries. You must convey confidence in what you do.

"For me, sponsorship has enabled my work to progress and will act as a recommendation of my abilities for future shows and to future funders. It can raise the standard of your work and, although it is sickening how important presentation has become, it is nevertheless crucial that the standard of work does not suffer through lack of funds. One drawback though is that it hides the way the government has devalued art, and forces artists into the role of market competitor.

"I would be cautious from whom I sought sponsorship, too, as it can be seen as a way of undermining an artist's independence – especially with more politically-oriented work – although this argument can equally be made against forms of state funding."

6 • Alternatives & opportunities

Lee Corner

Eighteen years ago a student was handed an envelope by his Royal College of Art professor (who often carried an A4 brown envelope of cash with which he would take students out for a meal, to an exhibition or whatever he felt they needed at the time). He knew this student was impoverished and, more importantly, out of sync with the London ethos that pervaded the college and the Cork Street mentality that underpinned most of the teaching. So, he gave him an envelope of cash and told him to get to Paris. There the student discovered Leger, the Pompidou Centre and a world where art unapologetically spilled into public spaces. The student decided that this was what he wanted to do. Having spent the intervening years developing and honing his practice, he has become an artist of considerable repute who works with and in public spaces.

Personal patronage of such a kind would be hard to find in art colleges of the 1990s, and this is no tale of rags to riches. But it is worth being reminded that the effect of an unexpected gesture can be out of all proportion to the act itself. Eighteen years ago it is highly unlikely that student – or any other – would have known how to find financial support for foreign travel, or for anything else, other than the college's own bursaries and awards. As he left college he would only have been aware of regional or national arts councils if one of his tutors served on an advisory panel. He would never have dreamt of looking for support from a local authority. Nowadays, the publicising of funding guidelines and the advertising of schemes has made it easier to know what is available while, at the same time, greater demand and the depletion of resources means there is less money to go round.

Developing a business

Artists are, on the whole, more entrepreneurial than they were two decades ago. Equally the funding system has been made more accessible. There are now shelves of books in libraries, ranging from directories of grant making trusts to step-by-step guides to sponsorship.

Advice

Regional arts boards often have staff whose job it is to help artists and arts organisations approach new sources of funding. West Midlands Arts, for example, houses a Business Development Unit which provides a range of services to artists and arts organisations.

Business in the Arts, an initiative of ABSA, encourages business people to help arts managers develop managerial capabilities through training, links with enterprise agencies and a placement scheme. Placements enable skilled business people to work as voluntary advisers, giving around 2-3 hours a fortnight to an organisation to help them with a challenging project. The aim is to pass on skills so arts organisations are better equipped to deal with similar situations in the future. See 9 • Contacts for regional offices.

These include:

- induction days – "to find the most creative solution to the problems that get in the way when trying to plan new projects"
- business development surgeries – "... covering any aspect of arts business management including finance, marketing, personnel or fundraising"
- training surgeries – "... including training needs analysis, training policies and constructive training approaches ...."
- sponsorship surgeries – "... all aspects of sponsorship including applications for the Business Sponsorship Incentive Scheme."

These are free services and operate alongside the various grants, bursaries and awards for specific projects including vocational or management training in Britain or abroad and marketing developments.

Loans and grants

Practical help and advice are also available from the extensive network of Prince's Youth Business Trust (PYBT) offices – 38 covering England, Wales and Northern Ireland, and a further network in Scotland. This charity which helps young people to set up or develop their own businesses has helped some 15,000 young people since its inception in 1987 and it reckons that two-thirds of businesses are still operational.

Jayne Knowles applied to them for a loan some 12 months after leaving the Combined Crafts course at Crewe and Alsager College (now part of Manchester Metropolitan University). She was awarded a £1000 loan and a £750 bursary – the latter for equipment and the former for anything to make the business viable. The smaller sum enabled her to buy a forge, steel cutting shears and business cards, and two years on she is successfully established in a studio in Essex where she makes candlesticks, clocks and other items in forged steel.

Though the money was undoubtedly important to her, Jayne believes the additional assistance given by PYBT was crucial. Most importantly the PYBT hall at the prestigious NEC International Autumn Fair – which specialises in trade crafts and giftware – gave her her first

Travel award

Cottage Garden, Gerry Copp.
Papier mâché vessel 38 x 11cm in recycled paper. Photo:
James Copp

Gerry Copp was awarded £2000 in 1993 by the St Hugh's Foundation Arts Scholarship fund towards costs of research and training into mosaic techniques and materials and to look at the potential of using recycled ceramics for outdoor public art. "I have developed working practices that allow me to use materials and processes which have minimal negative impact on the environment. Initally, I used waste fabrics to make rag rugs and have since explored and developed techniques using hand-made recycled paper to collage onto papier mâché formers. I now want to produce works suitable for public, outdoor locations. As paper is not appropriate, I have developed an interest in the potential of mosaics using recycled ceramics."

The award enabled her to consult London-based mosaicist Magnus Irvin, study Nikki de Saint Phalle's Tuscany Tarot Garden and also investigate possible sources of materials which could be recycled for use in outdoor works.

"The biggest lesson I have learned from the experience of applying for funding is to over-estimate the cost of a project as, with hindsight, I realise that my costs were not realistic for what I proposed doing."

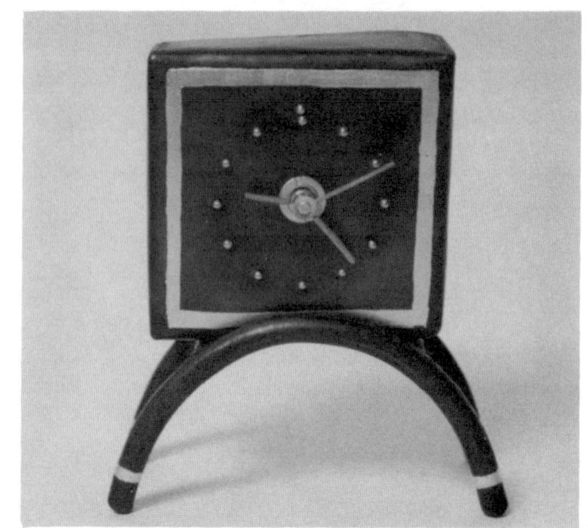

Square free-standing clock, 13cm tall in forged and welded steel with gold leaf by Jayne Knowles**. Photo:** the artist

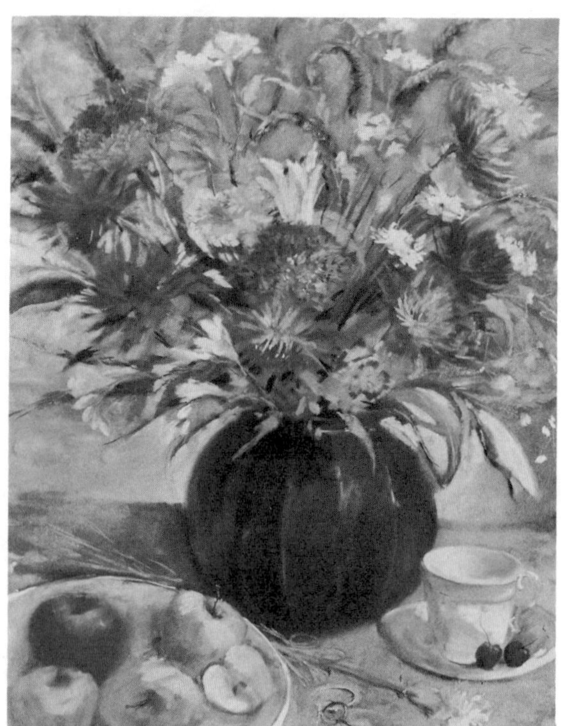

***Flowers, fruit and ruby vase*, a 24" x 38" painting in wash, pastel and chalk by** Nel Whatmore**. Photo:** the artist

two major retail outlets, and she has found her business adviser invaluable. She is now preparing a business plan to enable her to apply for a PYBT expansion loan, and welcomes their recent decision to extend the upper age limit to 29!

Nel Whatmore was one of the first artists to get a PYBT grant, which she received in 1986. She had tried to take advantage of other small firms advisory and starter schemes but had frequently found herself patronised and the butt of comments such as, "You can't be businesslike and an artist." She now serves as a business adviser for the trust because she recognises its importance as a body which takes risks and which takes artists seriously.

Nel Whatmore, who produces highly coloured figurative paintings, sells her still lives and landscape works to customers in the UK and abroad and also works closely with fine art publishers Washington Green. She also organises and self-finances an annual one-week exhibition of paintings and prints to which she invites a mailing list of 1000 previous and potential customers. A substantial amount of work – which ranges in price from £150 to £900 – is sold at the preview.

Travelling hopefully

Maybe it is something to do with being an island race that trade with other lands has always been considered exotic and only to be enjoyed by the privileged few. Up until our identity as a part of Europe became unavoidable most people still considered any form of travel as skiving off, and though some still do, there has been a marked change in the attitude of funders to travel grants in recent years. Now there are 'international initiatives' and 'new horizons' funds in most national and regional arts funding bodies and the opportunities listings in *Artists Newsletter* and other journals bulge with fellowships and scholarships offered by foundations in places such as the US, Japan, Scandinavia and Jamaica.

Membership of the European Community (EC) has opened up a wealth of funding opportunities though most potential applicants are put off by real or imagined paperwork and bureaucracy. *Finance From Europe* by Dr Michael Hopkins is a book produced by, and available from, the European Commission: "The European Commission recognises that increased investment in the development of human resources is vital if Europe is to take full advantage of the economic opportunities provided by the single market. In order to meet the education and training needs of the European economy and society the commission has devised a number of programmes relating to education, training and

New Horizons

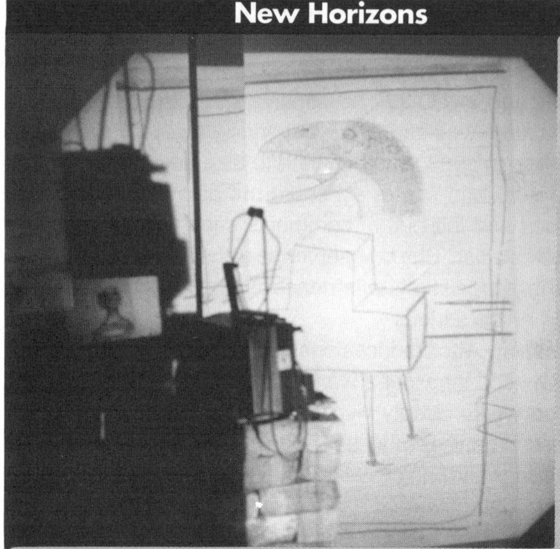

***Plato's Cave*, an installation by** Simon Lewandowski. **Photo:** the artist

Simon Lewandowski, an artist using traditional and computerised print techniques in his work, applied for a 1992 Gulbenkian Foundation New Horizons award, which sought proposals from artists wishing to extend the scope of their work by using new materials or techniques, or through collaboration with others.

He proposed to explore multi-media computer techniques, where sound, text and graphics are used to create interactive or other kinds of presentation. "My interest is to apply multi-media technology to a wider range of output forms, bringing the work out to world. Instead of interactive programmes controlling sound and image on screen, I would look at the possibility of controlling elements on a more theatrical and environmental scale using projection, lighting effects, automata and robotics on a one-to-one scale with the spectator. I plan to investigate new software, and look at technologies related specifically to a theatrical scale and make contact with a range of organisations in the UK and elsewhere including the San Francisco-based Survival Research Laboratories."

A £3000 award enabled him to test out relevant technologies, visit artists, critics and technologists in the USA, and look at the feasibility of producing an interactive electronic publication. *Plato's Cave*, an installation in May 1993 at Leeds Workspace, was the first piece of work to incorporate technical and narrative elements arising from the research.

"The research grant was invaluable, even just for the network- and contact-making. I had a reason to go to another country and cold-call people, using my research grant as credentials."

Knocking on doors

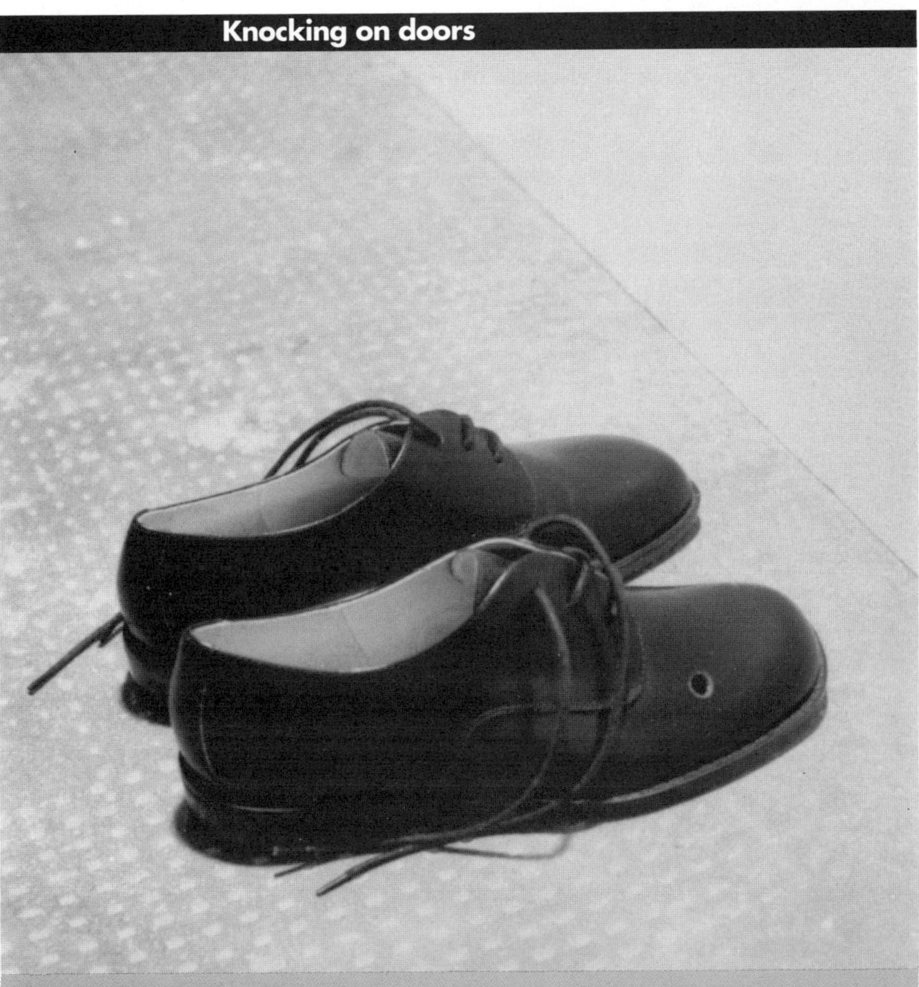

***Shoes with 9mm hole* by Christine Borland from 'Artists Show Artists' Galerie Vier, Berlin, 1992. Photo: Douglas Gordon**

In 1991, Christine Borland enrolled on a Goethe Institut German language course in Glasgow, discovering during the year that scholarships were available to selected students interested to study the language in Germany. Her application to study in the Berlin institute was successful and, as well as the two-month intensive language course, she was provided with accommodation in a flat, £40 a week pocket money and return flight.

Going in January/February 1992, once her German was good enough, she set about "knocking on doors", visiting the many galleries, alternative arts centres and studios in the Kreuzberg area, showing her work and also that of other artists and galleries in Glasgow. As a result, she was offered a studio in the Kunstlerhaus Bethanien (an international arts centre) for two months, which she took up in the summer of 1992. The artistic director of the Kunstlerhaus subsequently included her work in an 1993 exhibition which was shown in Potsdam, in former East Germany, paying her costs to come over and install the work.

She discovered that whilst in Germany she could continue claiming Housing Benefit for her Glasgow flat. This was possible because both visits to Germany were recognised as study or training situations which would increase her chances of getting employment in the future, and because she was not earning any money in Germany (her 'pocket money' was discounted as earnings). The HB office required letters from the institutions verifying the purposes of her visits and confirmation she was not earning money, as well as a letter from her Glasgow landlord confirming rent was paid. For the studio visit, a listing in the publication *Women in Arts: networking internationally* encouraged her to apply to the Kathleen and Margery Elliot Scholarships which assists educational exchange, and she received a grant of £100 towards expenses.

During 1993, Christine Borland has exhibited in Germany, at Venice Biennale, Second Tyne International in Newcastle upon Tyne and Chisenhale Gallery in London.

youth and has created a special Task Force for Human Resources, Education, Training and Youth to co-ordinate actions in these areas."

Information sources

There is no need for the artist to struggle single-handedly through the maze of information and acronyms – ERASMUS, IRIS, PETRA. Many higher and further education institutions have designated staff who understand the workings of different education and training programmes, and regional MEPs (Members of the European Parliament) are an often untapped source of information and practical assistance. In addition there are 21 European Information Centres across the UK providing an information and advice service on community policies and programmes, national legislation and business practices, and over forty European Documentation Centres which – though their primary function is to

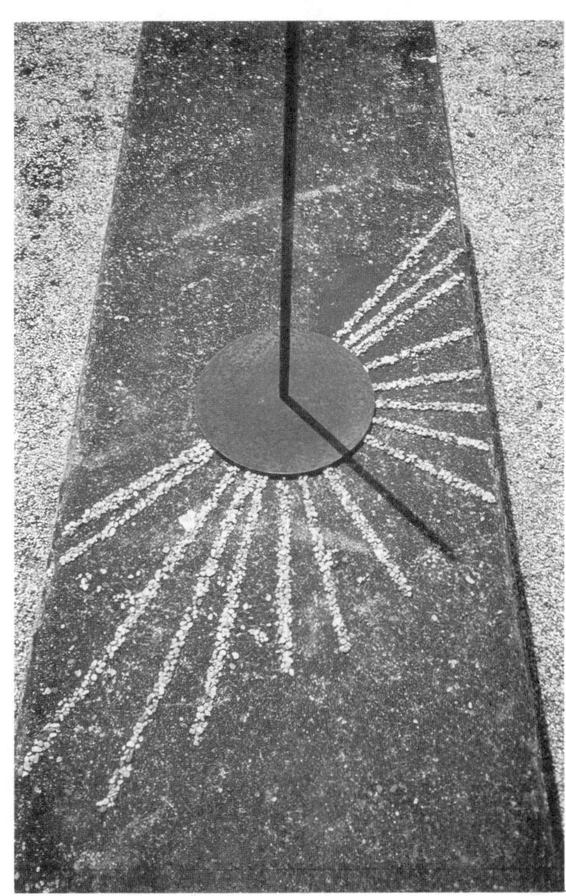

***1.30pm, 15th February, 1993, facing North East,* Tower Studio roof, Melbourne, from an installation by** Catherine Clover. **This gnomon or sundial is one of a series of six which evolved from living and working in the Southern Hemisphere. Through the position of the shadow, the gnomon indicates the opposite angle of the sun in the sky, and through the length and breadth of shadow, indicates the opposite season.**
Photo: the artist

stimulate and sustain the development of and the study of Europe – are charged to provide an EC information service to the wider community.

Taking chances

If existing travel schemes for Europe or beyond prove too restrictive, a more opportunist approach sometimes pays off. A chance conversation led Catherine Clover to discover that courier flights to Australia could be found for as little as £200. Catherine decided that at such a rate the chance to broaden her horizons and seek new opportunities was eminently affordable. Courier flights are the means by which some companies ensure personal and safe delivery of goods between countries. Information about them tends to be carried by word-of-mouth, but is also available through subscription to specialist journals which list them.

She took her slides to galleries in Sydney, Adelaide and Melbourne and from the latter secured the immediate offer of a studio residency for six months at 200 Gertrude Street – a state-funded art gallery also providing subsidised studios for 15 local and two overseas artists. Once she was there, Catherine's residency was extended to 15 months. She had no success at all in gaining funds from charitable trusts, the Commonwealth Institute, the British Council or her regional arts board but Spectrum Oil Colours donated £500 worth of materials and a prize of AUS$2000 in the Artworks Four open exhibition contributed to her subsistence costs. In addition, her 1500-square-foot Tower Studio located within Queens College was provided rent free.

Transferable skills

Sometimes being in another place itself provides the catalyst for a change of direction. Anny Evason was already living and working as a painter in Australia when a friend invited her to assist with the design of a show for the Women and Theatre Festival at the Nimrod Theatre, Sydney. As the work of a painter – rather than a set designer – the result was stylised, painterly and innovative and (probably for the same reasons) did not work entirely on a practical level. However, it caught the eye of the theatre's Artistic Director who encouraged her to apply for a Loudon Sainthill Design Scholarship.

Though the scholarship represented a comparatively small amount of money it offered Anny the opportunity of a year's paid training in Sydney working on new plays with some of Australia's leading theatre professionals. Moreover, it gave her a ten-year career in theatre design in Britain and Australia as well as a new set of skills, new methods of

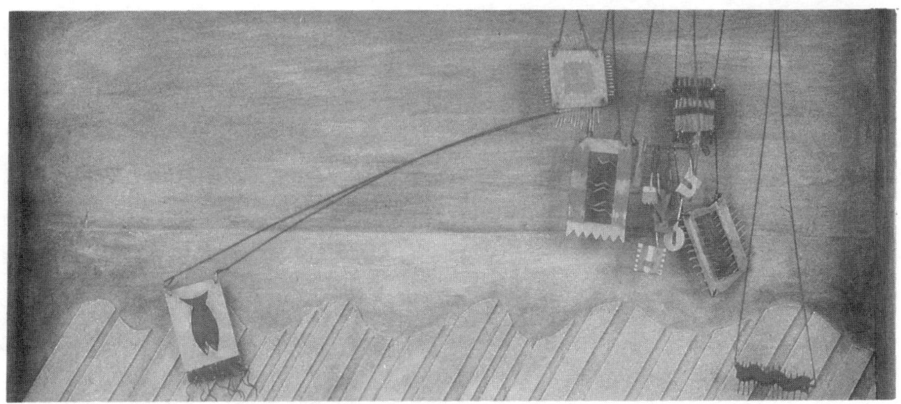

***Line, Lead, Plummet,* a 39x22x5cm painted construction in acrylic, wood and card by** Anny Evason. **Photo:** Othens Photographic Studio

working, and a different way of seeing – all of which she is now applying to her work as a painter back in the UK.

Thinking local

It's harder to think of opportunities in our immediate localities holding as much excitement as those which take us to distant lands, but Kate Russell has realised that it is her local community that is likely to provide her with most long-term security.

In 1992 Kate embarked on the planning for a major piece of work which – if she could raise the appropriate funding – would occupy her full time for the next five years. With a small grant from Leeds City Council she explored the feasibility of creating a 24-panel tapestry for the State Rooms of the Civic Hall celebrating the accomplishments of the different communities of Leeds for the occasion of its centenary.

Kate recognised that her need for information which would enable her accurately to represent the communities could be dovetailed with their interest in publicity (and accurate representation) to mutual benefit. For her first panel, therefore, she approached a number of firms of solicitors to 'buy into' the image of Leeds as England's second largest law city. A £500 investment would buy the chance to have the company's building or logo woven into the panel. Five firms took up the offer in the first three weeks and 50% of the funding for the first panel was secured.

The subsequent publicity has already brought enquiries from other sectors and Kate feels sure that by this method she will be able to fund this substantial work.

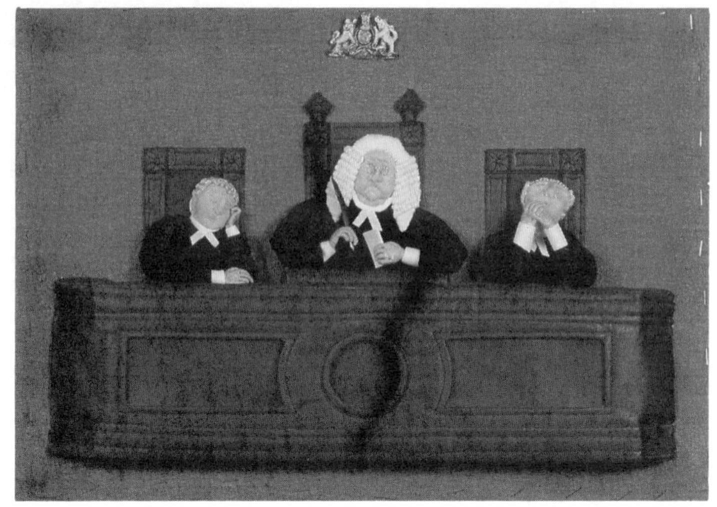

***Pro Rege et Lege*, the first of 24 panels for Leeds Civic Hall by** Kate Russell. **Photo:** the artist

Collaborations

Kate Russell had, to some extent, tested her ability to secure partnerships some years before when, forced into new ways of thinking about survival by the deepening recession, she approached a new marketing firm which had just established itself in Leeds. The company was run by two women and the proposal that Kate took to them was that in return for business and marketing advice she would make them a piece of work for their boardroom. "The directors were attracted by the novelty value of having a piece of original artwork. They recognised that it would be a conversation piece and that there were publicity opportunities in it for them. They paid generously for materials but we swapped our skills hour for hour – they gave me business advice and I worked on the boardroom piece."

Adam Reynolds has also found that partnerships and collaborations bring new resources. The Art Adviser for Thames Chase, the woodland management and development body whose remit covers parts of Essex and adjoining London boroughs, generated the idea of commissioning artists to make work for an access trail through an Essex community forest. As a result, Brentwood Borough Council has funded Adam to undertake the initial design stage, with realisation of the work likely to be funded by them in partnership with English Nature and other environmental organisations as well as by local businesses.

Hackney Contemporaries

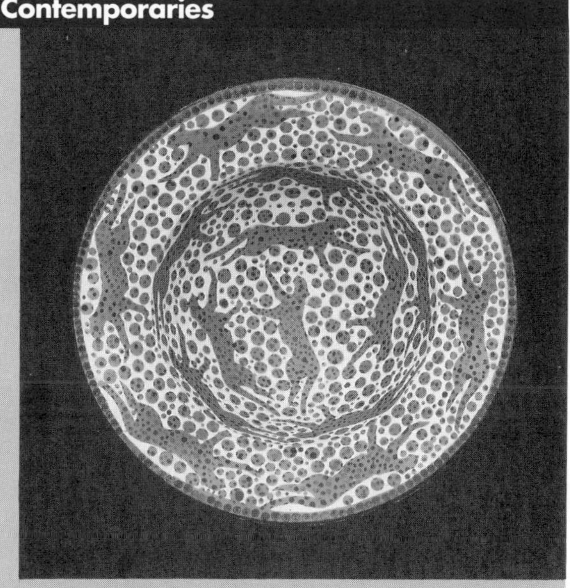

Cheetah bowl, **21cm diameter, by** Dimitra Grivellis. **Each of her porcelain pieces is sandblasted using a variety of resist-making materials and then decorated. Photo:** Anthony Oliver

The Hackney Contemporaries, whose launch exhibition was held at the Geffrye Museum in London in Autumn 1993, has gained financial and in-kind support for a move to promote Hackney and the skills of its designer-makers to new markets in the UK and Europe. The group's development has been co-ordinated by Dieneke Ferguson of Mazorca consultancy. She has raised £31,500 in money, as well as in-kind sponsorship such as business advice and sponsored publicity worth about £50,000, from Dalston City Challenge, CILNTEC (the training and enterprise council for the City, Islington and Hackney), East London Partnership, Hackney Enterprise into Europe, the Geffrye Museum, London Arts Board, the London Borough of Hackney and Momart. This includes sponsorship from the artists who not only donated their time but invested a percentage of sales income made through Hackney Contemporaries initiatives back into the venture. The offer of free exhibition space at LINEA, the international design show in Ghent, Belgium will be used to show furniture, ceramics, stained glass, mosaic, textiles, wall hangings rugs and hand-made furnishing trimmings of Kate Baden Fuller, Cressida Bell, Karen Bunting, Dimitra Grivellis, Celia Harrington, Fenella Mallalieu, Kate Malone, Susan Nemeth, Rebecca Newnham, Stemmer & Sharp, Frances Soubeyran, Jola Spytkowska and Sian Tucker. The group intends to become self-managing after the two-year setting-up period, and to raise funds to promote its work through a variety of European events and exhibitions.

It's not what you do...

A new, different or unusual source of funding is only such the first time someone takes advantage of it. All too soon it becomes part of the mainstream. Eighteen years ago it would have been extremely rare if not inconceivable for a disability organisation, a business development initiative, or even a city council to fund an artist or an arts project. Though funding is never easy to come by, it is almost certainly true that there are now more sources funding more people than ever before.

For artists in the nineties, career alternatives are fewer and it is likely to be their obsessive commitment which determines their survival, and which creates the motivation to search out yet another idea which may earn them a living. But commitment alone will not suffice: it must be matched with a confident and competent approach which convinces the funder that you're worth the investment.

Confidence and clarity

Kate Russell is convinced that her ability to persuade less obvious funders to support her work comes from a combination of confidence and clarity: "I've now got it clear what I do and how it differs from what other artists do. I am able to talk about it with passion and without pretension. I get a great deal of pleasure and fulfilment from producing work which satisfies and delights others and which takes in their vision as well as my own."

Working out what funders will respond to is the hardest task and it demands care and close preparation. In the case of the Prince's Youth Business Trust it may be a cash flow forecast and a business plan. In the case of a firm of solicitors it may be a little flattery and a professional presentation. But almost without exception, the way to unlock new sources of money is to unlock the imagination of a potential contributor or investor.

7 • On the receiving end

Brian Baker

What do funders and sponsors look for in a fundraising application? Although the fine detail varies, some administrators placing more emphasis on particular factors than others, some messages are universal: don't be sloppy and don't waste people's time.

Essential though good presentation is, there's more to maximising chances of success than neatness and legibility or evidence of research. Although most funders and sponsors are comfortable with neat handwriting for actual applications, where an artist-run organisation is applying for a substantial sum for a capital scheme, most require a business plan and this and the detailed supporting material are best produced on a typewriter or word processor.

Knowing exactly what you are applying for is crucial. Birmingham City Council's Community Arts Development Officer, Ann Moss, recalls with bemused horror experiences of artists applying for residencies openly saying that they only want to do it to "pay the rent". Whilst she and other funders feel that an artist's suitability for a project only really comes through at interview, written applications are crucial, because only three or four artists will be selected for the short-list from probably dozens of written applications.

Visual material

Most funders expect applications to contain relevant photographs or slides. The importance of effectively labelling material is emphasised, as this not only helps a selection panel to make sense of them, but ensures artists will get them back afterwards. However, artists need to think more carefully about what kind of supporting visual material will work best.

Cardiff Bay Art Trust Director Sally Medlyn is astonished at the number of applications which arrive accompanied by large-format transparencies which can only be viewed by holding them up to the light. Even artists well-experienced in public art commissions still do this. "I'm showing work at a pace in a darkened room to people with limited time. If I have to stop and pass round a 5" x4" transparency when all the other slides are in the projector, it doesn't help the artist concerned." Because of this, her agency now indicates on material sent out with the brief that 35mm slides are preferable.

Foundation for Sport and the Arts

The private organisation currently dealing with the largest number of applications and flow of funds is the Foundation for Sport and the Arts, established in the autumn of 1991 and funded through the Pools companies. Working "totally on paper", Secretary Grattan Endicott now has a team of 20 in offices near Walton in Liverpool, though in the early rounds of grant awarding there were only three staff. In devising its methods for dealing with applications, the foundation aims to keep administration costs down to less than 2% of budget.

Receiving over 300 applications a week, average spend per week in 1993/4 will be £1.2 million. Applications are assessed in three levels: bids for less than £25,000; bids for between £25,000 and £100,000 and those for larger amounts. The trust's deed – which designates that one third of available finance should be spent on the arts – is otherwise fairly unrestrictive, although for sport there are more constraints, for example it does not fund football schemes or pastimes which are cruel to animals. "We are looking for geographical and art-form spread in each tranche," says Endicott.

The foundation works on a rolling basis, grants being determined and confirmed as finance from Pools companies is received. This can mean a long wait, and often enthusiastic trustees get a little ahead of the flow.

A standard application form is used, and organisations and others applying for substantial sums are expected to send a detailed business plan as well. Grattan Endicott confirms, "We like to see applicants have taken proper professional advice where appropriate. It's part of a business-like approach." In addition to staff, the foundation uses professional advisers – accountants, and engineers for building schemes – who help to assess proposals. Endicott confirms "grants for individuals are rarely in four figures. We can give in the low thousands to individuals but this is much rarer. The circumstances must be wholly exceptional and be vouched by an individual of high repute."

"Crispness of presentation is key," he says. "People who send us beautifully produced volumes would be disappointed at how little

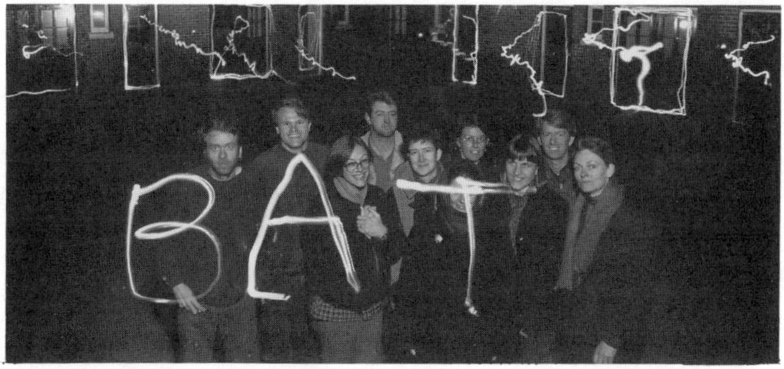

Birmingham Art Trust artists performing a nocturnal event outside the studios to launch an open studios weekend. Photo: Gary Kirkham

Birmingham Art Trust launched their 'Getting Started' scheme in 1989 after winning the enthusiastic support of Marks & Spencer who were the major sponsors. They backed it for three years at around £5000 a year, enabling BAT to award three bursaries annually. Selected in open competition, these were worth £1500 each and were open to young or recently graduated artists. The artists were provided with studio space and general advice and were otherwise expected to arrange their own programme, centred around collaborative projects with established artists or artist-run organisations. Marks & Spencer's only condition was that artists should have been educated in the UK. BAT expected them to be based in the Birmingham area for the year. Elizabeth Callender says, "I went and saw Birmingham Art Trust and realised they were artists with a really good idea and that they knew how to realise it." She spent time discussing the programmes and development of the artists' business skills. Several artists who took part in the scheme did residencies during their year, and others travelled to studios of artists they admired and worked with them, most gaining in experience and self-confidence as a result.

attention they attract. And those who send us videos will be upset that we have no time to watch them." Not everyone finds videos a problem though. Both Ann Moss and Gateshead Borough Council's Visual Arts Officer, Anna Pepperall, don't, finding them a useful adjunct to written applications, and are prepared to view any sent.

Marks & Spencer

Like Endicott, Marks & Spencer's Elizabeth Callender, Manager of Community Affairs, highlights the importance for established arts organisations of submitting accounts and business plans. A member of Business in the Community's long-term planning committee, she has been at M&S for nine years, and has seen substantial changes in arts funding over recent years. Her department now receives about 20,000 enquiries a year, though not all relate to the arts.

Their policy is that they usually try to meet with first time applicants if they are asking for more than about £3000. Whilst Marks & Spencer doesn't often fund exhibitions, in considering an exhibition's application, Callender would "want to know how it would be promoted, where it would be going, how the work would be selected and, if it were touring, to satisfy ourselves that the budget was realistic."

Research

Ann Moss emphasises how crucial it is that artists applying for community-based residencies should understand the field of work. Artists working in such situations "need to subscribe to the community arts philosophy, and want to use their creativity to unlock other people's." Although they advertise large residencies in *Artists Newsletter* and *MailOut,* they also keep a file of artists interest in a particular type of work and they are mailed appropriate job briefs.

Last year she arranged student placements with two major residencies. Planned in advance, students were interviewed by the community groups in charge of the projects, just as the artists had been. Ann Moss also points out that "student placements look good on a graduate's CV."

When looking at applications, Moss looks "for evidence of voluntary work because for my projects, artists have got to have a passion to enable people to do things." Anna Pepperall also processes a wide range of applications – from bids for an exhibition or a residency to proposals for support with a project idea. In respect of artists' initiatives, "we prefer artists to contact us initially to demonstrate commitment. We usually ask artists to come and outline the idea in person." They then look for evidence of follow-up research. "We aren't impressed if they come back with the same proposal we discussed in the first conversations." She emphasises Gateshead's willingness to be pro-active, and despite the cuts, this approach is mirrored in other local authorities.

Prince's Trust

Anne Engel, Project Director of the Prince's Trust Partners in Europe initiatives, runs the Go & See and Go Ahead schemes, sponsored by Severn Trent plc. Over 60% of Go & See funds are now taken up by art, craft and design projects. "It is a very small grant: airline ticket and £200 or £300 for people under 26 to go and meet a person in another country

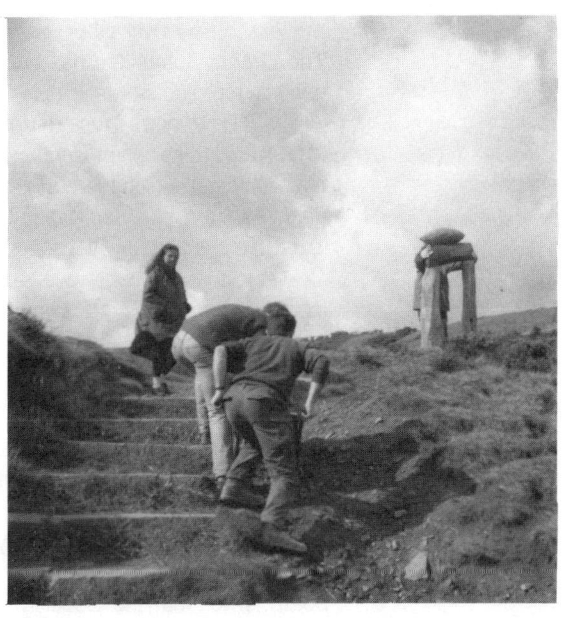

Mirna Arsovska **installing *Good Morning Anglia*, a 66" x 30" x 12" sculpture in wood on the Huddersfield Canal in Mossley. Photo:** Kerry Morrison

Kerry Morrison got a Go Ahead grant from the Prince's Trust Partners in Europe programme in 1992. It followed her 1991 Go and See award when she had gone to Macedonia in former Yugoslavia shortly after the war broke out. As a result, she remained in Skopje for her two-week visit. Struck by the similarities between the work of artists she met there and that of her contemporaries here, she was "fired up to bid for Go Ahead." She linked the idea of bringing Macedonian artists with an idea she had for creating site-specific sculpture in Tame Valley along the Huddersfield Canal. "I put a lot of time and thought into the application", preparing a detailed budget which included daily costs such as food. The result was that she secured £3000 from Partners in Europe and £2000 from North West Arts, with Tameside Metropolitan Borough Council providing assistance in kind in various ways. Kerry Morrison selected three artists to visit for nine weeks in the summer of 1992, choosing those she felt would adapt well. The pool of funds and work opportunities were boosted when Oldham Metropolitan Borough Council commissioned her to do some sculpture in Alexander Park that summer. "I was able to bring two of the Macedonian artists into that project. We put all of the money into a pot and divided it."

and make connections across Europe." The maximum grant is £500, and the upper age limit is slightly higher for people with disabilities. There is a standard application form, and about 150 small grants are awarded a year. Go Ahead grants are designed to follow on from Go & See and enable projects to be fully realised, with about 20 grants of up to £5000 each awarded annually.

Anne Engel emphasises "we are not judges of artistic quality" and that they do not want supporting visual material initially. "Our arts support is about working with other people. The basic objective is to enable young people early in their working life to experience working in a different culture with other people." But "Initiatives have to be innovatory. The Grants Committee has become reluctant to accept straight joint exhibition projects."

The Prince's Trust 'Partners in Europe' administers the Richard Mills Travel Fellowships and a new competition, European Vision. The fellowships, of which there are three a year, are currently worth £1000 each. As there is no application form, artists are guided by the Prince's Trust in making applications. The European Vision competition selects 12 winners a year, who receive £2000 each for a month's stay and a language course in the European city of their choice.

Guidelines

Like most local authorities, Gateshead's guidelines rule out grants to individuals though there are some exceptions. "Sometimes we cover travel and opportunities to work for people who have been working with us already in our twin towns," says Anna Pepperall.

Local authorities often advise individuals to try the regional arts board, who, with the Scottish and Welsh arts councils, remain an important source not only of funding but of advice for visual artists. East Midlands Arts Fine Arts Officer Janet Currie, says "we turn round applications from receipt to notification usually in 4-6 weeks. It takes longer if advisers defer a decision for further information." For start-up scheme grants – a maximum of £500 for artists just starting out – an application form is used, although for all of their other grant programmes, aimed at individual artists and artists' groups, applicants have to produce their own proposals based on extensive and detailed guidelines. For bids from artists' groups, "we want to see some background: business plans and accounts information is important, especially for organisations applying for a second year of support."

Time-scales

As Anna Pepperall selects work for her exhibition programme at specific times of year, she sometimes keeps artists' work and proposals for two months or more, although "with residencies and project ideas the waiting period can be longer."

Foundation for Sport and the Arts grants are largely determined in advance of trustee meetings which have a policy emphasis. Extensive use is made of fax machines and the trustees study assessments on applications and form views beforehand.

Whilst hassling on the telephone does applicants no good at all, the message is don't give up if you don't succeed initially. "Whilst we have to say to so many we can't stretch the money at a particular time, we don't necessarily turn people down for ever," says Grattan Endicott.

At Marks & Spencer, where the total spend on Arts, Community Arts and Heritage last year was £700,000 spread across 210 donations, larger grants are determined three times a year by an internal committee so there can be a wait, but other decisions are monthly, applicants being told the results within 4-6 weeks as far as possible.

Matching funding

Matching money need not necessarily be in the form of cash. There are many examples of sponsorship in kind of materials or services being used to match grants. See also Sponsorship in kind.

A general view is that artists should check out all potential funders as early as possible, and that multiple funding is advantageous. Elizabeth Callender says, "We will often give half if they can find the other half, and an agreement from us will often encourage another sponsor." At Gateshead, the policy is to suggest organisations they might approach. Anna Pepperall says, "For extensive schemes, we expect them to make applications for finance to the other sources." At the Foundation for Sport and the Arts, Grattan Endicott finds, "It encourages trustees when applicants have made the effort to find funds from elsewhere." Janet Currie at East Midlands Arts agrees. She usually suggests other possible funders at an early stage and encourages groups to pursue several funding sources in parallel.

Selection

At the interview stage Sally Medlyn says, "Although it's difficult, artists should try to relax and be themselves. The ones who come over really well are those who calmly and unpretentiously take us through every aspect of the project."

For charities and community sponsors, interviews to decide on smaller grants are often with local representatives. Marks & Spencer uses store managers, but the Prince's Trust has a network of 63 local groups. Both Anne Engel and Elizabeth Callender urge artists to remember these people are not experts. They do not want to be mystified by complex visual arts information.

Follow-up

Most funders require a report when they have grant-aided a project. Anne Engel says, "We ask specific questions. The reports artists produce are usually very good." Ann Moss says, "We like artists to be involved in monitoring and evaluation of projects. Sometimes I ask them to write a report pointing out strengths and weaknesses in a project as they perceive them." Anna Pepperall says, "At the end of a long-term residency or other major project we require a written report as part of the contract, although it's not necessary for shorter residencies."

But at East Midlands Arts, "We expect a written report for every grant we make." If Janet Currie hasn't received it by the beginning of the final quarter of the year she writes to grant recipients requesting one.

Turn-off

What puts off recipients of fundraising applications? For Elizabeth Callender of Marks & Spencer, it is "multiple applications from the same organisation addressed to different people all over the business." She also "gets the horrors when people in arts organisations patently can't spell." Janet Currie has two particular dislikes. "People who don't read the guidelines", and applications from "artists who don't really seem to know what they want to do." Anne Engel is put off by "pretentious, overblown statements about what artists do or, worse, what they think. We don't want to know what they think."

Sally Medlyn recalls, "I had a situation where an artist came not having prepared a costing. That left us unable to make a decision." She also dislikes the minority who put forward maquettes and proposals devised for another commission. "Having sold the idea of a site-specific work to my commissioner it counts against an artist if they offer off-the-shelf pieces."

Impressive

All funders are impressed by the general improvement in artists' presentational skills, notably those of younger artists. Notwithstanding this, Anne Engel is critical of the education system. "Art departments should be doing 100% more to assist students in practical skills." Whilst emphasising the importance of linguistics in applying for their schemes, more generally she feels "what's important with us is that you apply for something you genuinely want to do."

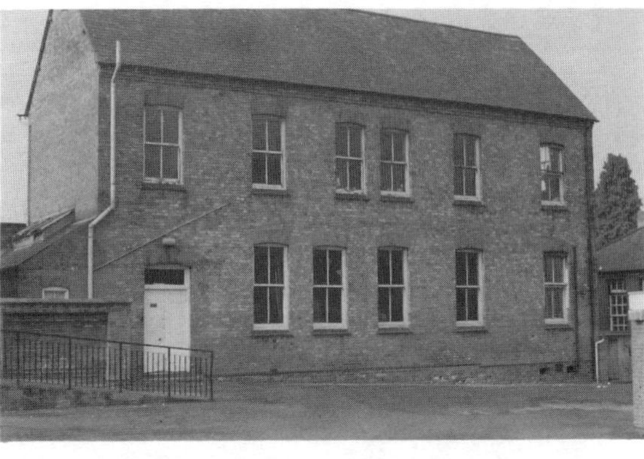

Rear of Knighton Lane Studios, Leicester. Photo: Knighton Lane Studios

Leicester-based Knighton Lane Group secured a £1300 grant from East Midlands Arts in 1993 for the first phase of a scheme to establish in the city an artists' resource for preparation of exhibitions. The artist-run studio group envisage the resource evolving over a two to three-year time span, so it can be evaluated and adjusted at each stage. In the first year, key equipment like hand-tools and a circular saw are being obtained, an extractor fan has been installed and training for using the equipment initiated. In addition to individual artists in the East Midlands, smaller galleries are likely to use the resource. The EMA panel assessing the application were impressed by clear evidence that health and safety, income generation, access, publicity and prioritising had all been properly addressed. Janet Currie says, "I was pleased also that they said in the first application what the cost of any further bids would be and why." The resource was scheduled to be in regular use by November 1993. Treasurer Paul Wood reports the budget was stretched by judicious purchasing skills. For example, one major piece of equipment was obtained for below catalogue price because they asked for a discount.

Elizabeth Callender sums up: "That they know who they are writing to; that an application is succinctly put together and that there is a clear budget. Where the application comes from an existing organisation like a studio group, it should include a set of accounts. With new organisations, we want to see a business plan." For Grattan Endicott at the Foundation for Sport and the Arts, "the essential thing is to present the material with clarity and crispness and give us a chance to take it in. It's important to fill in our questionnaire fully and to give a clear background of the organisation and to set out the project's objectives."

For Anna Pepperall, "Good presentation definitely helps: photographs are often better than slides. I look for evidence of thought and research appropriate to the project." Janet Currie is "impressed by people who express themselves with clarity and have a properly calculated budget." She welcomes applicants who can say with surety how much they need to achieve their goals.

David Canter Memorial Trust

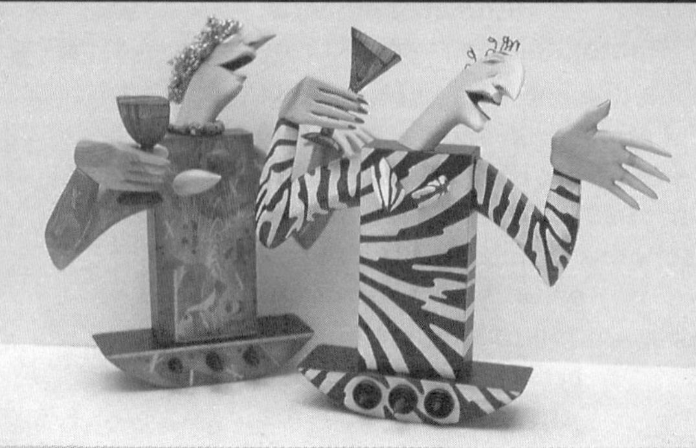

Drunken women rocking, 12" high by Eleanor Glover, 1993. Photo: the artist

"In my application to the David Canter Memorial Trust, I explained that my extremely old (at least 35 years) bandsaw – essential in roughing out shapes and making boxes – was not only noisy but could not cut square or straight. I asked for money towards a new one. I was successful, and selling the old one made up the full cost of the new bandsaw."

The David Canter Memorial Trust, set up five years ago to help craftspeople advance their careers, gives grants annually for travel, research, equipment or materials or a combination of these. In 1992, they got 300 applications. "As we haven't the resources to help everyone, we operate a filter system to eliminate in the first instance the uncommitted and obvious opportunists. We achieve this by careful study of a deceptively simple question on our application form: 'If you receive an award, how would you spend it?'

"From the replies, it is obvious many candidates are still working out their reply as they write, with corrections and crossings out common-place. It is also difficult to take seriously applications for equipment which are basically a shopping list with basic tools costing less than £15 which even the least committed beginner would already have.

"We are less favourably inclined to requests made on purely commercial grounds: a viable business looking to expand should be able to put that case to a bank. Grants for travel have to convince us of their integrity: we are not keen to fund inspirational holidays nor requests for travel grants to visit exotic places to see work we know to be in the V&A or Museum of Mankind. A plan to share knowledge of a research grant we regard more favourably, and applicants who are willing to make a contribution to the project have a definite advantage.

"Successful short-listed candidates are those who clearly demonstrate commitment and need. Their applications show clarity of purpose and proper costings which are well-presented and legible."

From an article on the David Canter Trust by Andy Christian and David Winkley, *Artists Newsletter*, December 1992

Sally Medlyn advises artists "to respond to the brief and not just send information about their work. In their approach, they need to indicate how they would approach and carry through the project." Ann Moss agrees that "applications should look like the artist has spent some time thinking why they want to do the project."

Advice

When making fundraising applications to arts officers and trust administrators their advice is to:

- do your research thoroughly
- include all relevant information in a formal application because funding bodies can't guarantee to come back and ask for more
- approach funders early for preliminary discussions about applications for funding for large schemes
- present your information well in the format most appropriate for each funding body to which you apply
- set out to raise funds only for projects you really want to do.

8 • Further reading

Books are listed by publisher, followed by distribution address and title of book. Many of these books will be found in public or education institute libraries or in resource and information centres.

ABSA

Available from: ABSA, Nutmeg House, 60 Gainsford St, Butlers Wharf, London SE1 2NY, tel 0171 378 8143.

Business Sponsorship Incentive Scheme. A leaflet explaining how the scheme works.

AN Publications

Available from: AN Publications, PO Box 23, Sunderland SR4 6DG, tel 0191 514 3600. Postage £1.50 per order.

Across Europe – the artist's personal guide to travel and work, 1st edition, ed. David Butler, 1992, ISBN 0 907730 15 9. Artists' experiences of exhibiting, living and working in 24 European countries. Also contains lists of contacts, resources and background information on each country. Price £9.95.

Directory of Exhibition Spaces, 4th edition, ed. Janet Ross, 1995, ISBN 0 907730 27 2. Lists over 2100 galleries and exhibition spaces in the UK, including public and private galleries, museums, libraries, arts centres, universities, theatres, heritage and community centres. Price £13.99.

Fact Pack: Insurance, 1993. Comprehensive information on artists' insurance needs. Price £1.85 inc p&p.

Fact Pack: Rates of Pay, 1993. Digest of fees and rates of pay for artists for commissions, residencies, workshops and exhibitions. Price £1.85 inc p&p.

Fact Pack: Slide Indexes, 1993. Listing 40 indexes and registers nationally, with details of eligibility and who consults them. Price £1.85 inc p&p.

Fact Pack: Artists and the EU, 1993. Contact list for all countries in Europe. Price £1.85 inc p&p.

Health & Safety: making art and avoiding dangers, Challis & Roberts, 1991, ISBN 0 907730 10 8. Practical information and advice on health and safety for all involved in the creation of art and craftwork including substances, processes and equipment. Price £7.25.

Making Ways: the visual artist's guide to surviving and thriving, 3rd edition, ed. David Butler, 1992, ISBN 0 907 73016 7. Covers exhibiting, selling, working in public and with people, collective action, skill sharing, publicity and promotion, studios, health and safety, employment and legal issues, insurance, contracts and copyright with reading and contacts lists. Price £11.99.

Money Matters, 2nd edition, Sarah Deeks, Richard Murphy & Sally Nolan, 1995, ISBN 0 907730 26 4. Artist's financial guide to self-employment covering taxation, VAT, NIC. Includes accounting system devised especially for artists and makers. Price £7.25.

Organising Your Exhibition, 2nd edition, Debbie Duffin, 1991, ISBN 0 907730 14 0. Practical guide to setting up and organising exhibitions. Price £7.25.

Selling, Judith Staines, 1933, ISBN 0 907730 19 1. Practical advice, based on artists' experiences, of promoting and selling art and craft work. Price £7.25.

Arts Council

Available from: Arts Council, 14 Great Peter Street, London SW1P 3NQ.

An Introductory Guide to Travel Opportunities for Black Art Practitioners, Susan Okokon, 1991. Lists organisations, trusts and educational opportunities, although as it was produced in 1991, some information is now out-of-date. Price £5 inc p&p.

Arts Networking in Europe, Rod Fisher, 1992. Contact names, addresses and information of more than 140 European arts networks including some relevant to visual arts. Price £10 inc p&p.

Who Does What in Europe, Rod Fisher, ISBN 0 7287 0603 X. Listings and contacts for EC schemes, Council of Europe, UNESCO, foundations and other useful organisations. Price £7.50 inc p&p.

Associated Management Services

Available from: Associated Management Services, Grant Guide Department, 10 Broad Street, Swindon, Wilts SN1 2DR.

Guide to Grants for Business, 5th edition, 1993. Covers UK Government grants and loans, EC grants and includes local contacts. Price £39.50 plus postage.

Association of Illustrators

Available from: AN Publications, PO Box 23, Sunderland SR4 6DG, tel 0191 514 3600.

Survive: the illustrator's guide to a professional career, ed. Aidan Walker, 1988. The complete survival guide for illustrators. Price £9 plus £1.50 postage.

British American Arts Association

Available from: BAAA, 116 Commercial Street, London E1 6NF, tel 0171 247 5385.

The Artist in the Changing City, 1st edition, Williams, Bollen, Gidney & Owens, 1993, ISBN 09514763 1 9. Includes contacts list internationally for artists' workspaces. Price £11.45 inc p&p.

British Council

Available from: British Council, 10 Spring Gardens, London SW1A 2BN.

Studying Abroad, 1993. Leaflet briefly outlining schemes administered by the British Council and referring to other sources of information and publications. Free.

CAFE

Available from: CAFE, 23-5 Moss Street, Dublin 2 Ireland, tel [00 353] 1 671 3268.

Irish Funding Handbook, ed. Leonie Baldwin, 1993. Guide to funding for community and voluntary groups covering statutory, trust and company grant sources. Price £10 inc p&p.

Charities Aid Foundation

Available from: Publications Department, Charities Aid Foundation, 48 Pembury Road, Tonbridge, Kent TN9 2JD.

Directory of Grant-Making Trusts, 1993. Biannual, includes principle fields of interest of grant-making trusts in the UK; lists specific purpose and amounts of grants. Alphabetical register of grant-making organisations, with basic information. Price £53.80 inc p&p.

Commission of the European Communities

Available from: UK Office of the EC, Jean Monnet House, 8 Storey's Gate, London SW1P 3AT, tel 0171 973 1992.

Finance from Europe – guide to grants and loans from European Community, Michael Hopkins, 1991. Free.

Crafts Council

Available from: Crafts Council, 44a Pentonville Road, London N19HF, tel 0171 278 770.

Running a Workshop: Basic business for craftspeople, 2nd edition, ed. Barclay Price, 1989, ISBN 0 903798 80 8. Aimed at craftspeople, chapters cover exhibiting, selling, costing, premises, and administration of a craft workshop. Price £7.50 plus £2 postage.

Department of Trade and Industry

Tel 0181 200 1992.

Single Market, 1993. Set of publications including *Guide to Sources of Advice* and *Europe Open to Professionals.* Free.

Directory of Social Change

Available from: Directory of Social Change, 24 Stephenson Way, London NW1 2DP, tel 0171 209 5151, fax 0171 209 5044. Postage £2.50 per order.

Arts Sponsorship Handbook, 1st edition, David Fishel, 1993, ISBN 1 873860 09 9. Aims to help arts organisations to make the best of sponsorship opportunities, covering the implications and benefits and discusses how to develop a relationship with potential sponsors. Price £7.50.

Charitable Status: a practical handbook, 4th edition, Andrew Phillips, 1994, ISBN 1 873860 14 5. Covers registration, limits to policies, campaigning, tax relief and pitfalls. Price £7.95.

Environmental Grants 1993, 1st edition, Stephen Woollett, 1993, ISBN 0 907164 92 7. Guide to grants from government, companies and trusts for environmental work. Price £14.95.

Guide to Grants for Individuals in Need, 4th edition, ed. David Casson and Paul Brown, 1994, ISBN 1 873860 45 5. Covers 2000 charities concerned with individual poverty. Price £15.95.

Guide to the Major Trusts Vol 1, 5th edition, ed. Susan Fitzherbert, Luke Fitzherbert, 1994, ISBN 1 873860 49 8. Policies and practices of 300 major trusts making grants of over £150,000 a year. Details of each trust's background, interests and priorities. Price £15.95.

Guide to the Major Trusts Vol 2, ed. Forrester, Casson and Brown, 1995, ISBN 1 873860 64 1. Covers 700 trusts making grants of over £40,000 a year with policies, practices and examples of donations made, includes sources of information and advice. Price £15.95.

London Grants Guide, 2nd edition, ed. Lucy Stubbs, 1992, ISBN 0 907164 85 4. Covers grants for individuals and charities in London. Price £12.50.

Major Companies Guide, 3rd edition, ed. David Casson, 1994, ISBN 1 873860 22 6. Information on 400 major companies with policies, arts sponsorship and advice on applying. Price £14.95.

The Arts Funding Guide, Anne Marie Doulton, 1994, ISBN 1 873860 31 5. Practical advice for arts organisations on raising money from Arts Councils, RABs and other bodies, with details of local authority funding, grant-making trusts and business sponsorship. Also covers funds available from Europe and USA. Price £15.95.

The Complete Fundraising Handbook, 2nd edition, Sam Clarke, 1993, ISBN 1 873860 21 8. Deals with how to set about to raise funds, sources and types of funds available, different fundraising techniques, examples of good practice, list of contacts for help and advice. Price £12.95.

West Midlands Grants Guide, ed. Nicola Eastwood and Darren Felgate, 1991, ISBN 0 907164 78 1. Price £9.95.

Writing Better Fundraising Applications, Michael Norton, 1992, ISBN 0 907164 66 8. Step-by-step guide to planning and producing fundraising applications with advice on budgeting and communication skills. Price £9.95.

Eurocreation Association

Available from: 3 rue Debelleyme, 75003 Paris, France tel [00 33] 1 48 04 78 79.

Eurocreation Newsletter. Published ten times a year in French and English with articles and listings on Eurocreation schemes and others including Pepinieres for young artists. Ask for subscription rates.

Eurofi plc

Available from: Eurofi, Guildgate House, Pelican Lane, Newbury RG13 1NX tel 01635 31900.

Guide to European Community Grants & Loans, Comprehensive manual as a loose-leaf folder with update sheets. Price £140 annual subscription.

Europa Publications

International Foundation Directory, ed. Hodson, ISBN 09 46653 66 6. Lists international charitable foundations. Price £70.

Friends of the Earth and Directory of Social Change

Available from: Directory of Social Change, Radius Works, Back Lane, London NW3 1HL.

Finding Sponsorship for Community Projects – a step-by-step guide, Caroline Gillies, 1990, ISBN 0 907164 54 4. Includes who to approach, ethical guidelines, case studies and sources of information. Price £9.45 inc p&p.

German Academic Exchange Service

Available from: German Academic Exchange Service (DAAD), 17 Bloomsbury Square, Lonodn WC1A 2LP.

Scholarships & Funding for Study & Research in Germany. Annual guide for British academic staff, researchers and students on their schemes and those offered by others, with eligibility and deadlines.

HMSO

Available from: HMSO Bookshop Agents – see Yellow Pages

Study Abroad – UNESCO, 1992, ISBN 923 00 27154. Biennial guide to grants and awards for overseas study. Price £14.

Institute of International Education

Available from: 809 UN Plaza, New York, NY 10017, USA.

Handbook on US Study for Foreign Nationals

Kogan Page

European Community Education, Training and Research Programmes, ed. Preston, 1991, ISBN 0 7494 0438 8.

European Community Funding for Business Development, ed. European Policy Research Centre, 1991, ISBN 0 7494 0396 9. Guide to sources, grants and application procedures. Price £50.

Practical Sponsorship, Stuart Turner, ISBN 1 85091 245 9. Looks at the issue from the sponsor's and the recipient's viewpoints, emphasising that both parties should be aware of the other's needs. Price £12.95.

MacMillan

The Grants Register. Lists research and project grants, scholarships, fellowships, exchange opportunities primarily for postgraduate students for further professional or advanced vocational training.

National Council for Voluntary Organisations

Available from: National Council for Voluntary Organisations, Regent's Wharf, 8 All Saints Street, London N1 9RL, tel 0171 713 6161.

Grants from Europe, Ann Davison & Bill Sealy, 1993, ISBN 0 71991304 7. Lists EC grants, gives advice on raising money and influencing policy. Not specifically for the arts. Price £9.95.

Voluntary but Not Amateur, Forbes, Hayes & Reason, 1990. Guide to the legal aspects of running a small organisation, including fundraising and accounting. Price £7.95.

Reed Information Services

Key British Enterprises. Annual guide to Britain's top companies.

Research Training Initiatives

Funding Digest. Up-to-date information on new sources of money gleaned by scanning 140 key journals and analysing business sponsorship. Copies can usually be consulted at regional arts boards and art organisations.

Scottish Council for Voluntary Organisations

Available from: Scottish Council for Community Organisations, 18/19 Claremont Crescent, Edinburgh EH7 4QD.

Constitutions and Charitable Status, ISBN 1 870904 02 8. Simple, comprehensive handbook for those seeking charitable status in Scotland, containing information for committee members on constitutions and commonly-used models. Price £10 inc p&p.

Grants and Funds in Scotland, 3rd edition, 1992. Directory covering 400 charitable trusts with funds available to organisations and individuals in Scotland. Price £7.50 inc p&p.

Small Business Research Centre

Available from: Small Business Research Centre, Kingston University, Kingston Hill, Surrey KT2 7LB, tel 0181 547 7247.

Directory of Soft Loan Schemes for Small Businesses in England, 1st edition, ed. Martina Klett, 1993. Lists 58 sources for 'soft' loans (terms or conditions more favourable than normal market rates) for small firms. Training and other support is often available to help borrowers use finance effectively. Price £25.

South West Arts Board

Available from: AN Publications, PO Box 23, Sunderland SR4 6DG, tel 0191 514 3600.

Making Connections: the craftsperson's guide to Europe, Judith Staines, 1992, ISBN 0 95069 919 5. Sourcebook to guide makers through the maze of 'Euro-paperwork'. Includes selective listings of contacts and organisations in 15 European countries and World Crafts Council's Europe Directory. Price £5 inc p&p.

Times Books

Times 1000 – World's Top Companies. Address lists included.

Wales Council for Voluntary Action

Wales Council for Voluntary Action, Llys Ifor, Crescent Road, Caerphilly, Mid-Glamorgan CF8 1XL.

Wales Funding Handbook, 2nd edition, Tracy Jones, 1992/93, ISBN 1 8710 94 11 9. Comprehensive step-by-step guide to raising money for community and voluntary organisations in Wales. Price £5 inc p&p.

Women in Arts/Women Artists Slide Library

Available from: Women Artists Slide Library, Fulham Palace, Bishop's Avenue, London SW6 6EA tel 0171 731 7618.

Women in the Arts – Networking Internationally, 1991, ISBN 0 7287 0632 6. Articles and information on international travel, exchange and opportunities for women, with international listing of women in the arts. Price £3.

9 • Contacts

This section provides main contacts for advice, information and training. In the case of bodies offering grants, for space reasons we have only listed those listed in the book (see *Further reading* for books providing details of funding sources). Note, also that several organisations listed under 'Grants and advice' or 'Information' may also offer training. The 'Training' list there therefore includes only those organisations not mentioned elsewhere.

Councils & boards

Arts Council, 14 Great Peter Street, London, SW1P 3NQ, tel: 0171 333 0100. Only funds projects and programmes of 'national significance' including research and touring exhibitions. From April 1994 becomes Arts Council of England.

Arts Council of Northern Ireland, 185 Stranmillis Road, Belfast, BT9 5DU, tel: 01232 381 591. Funded by the Office of Northern Ireland.

BFI (Production Division), 29-35 Rathbone St, London, W1P 1AG, tel: 0171 636 5587, fax: 0171 580 9456. Information on UK and European funds including grants to regional film and video makers.

Crafts Council, 44a Pentonville Road, London, N1 9HF, tel: 0171 278 7700. Provides setting-up grants for individuals, subsidy for touring exhibitions. Comprehensive information service available by letter, telephone or in person.

East Midlands Arts Board, Mountfields HouseForest Road, Loughborough, LE11 3HU, tel: 01509 218292. Covers Leicestershire, Nottinghamshire, Northamptonshire and Derbyshire except High Peak District.

Eastern Arts Board, Cherry Hinton Hall, Cherry Hinton Road, Cambridge, CB1 4DW, tel: 01223 215355. Covers Bedfordshire, Cambridge, Essex, Hertfordshire, Lincolnshire, Norfolk, Suffolk.

London Arts Board, Elme House, 133 Long Acre, London, WC2E 9AF, tel: 0171 240 1313. Covers Greater London.

North Wales Arts Association, 10 Wellfield House, Bangor, Gwynedd, LL57 1ER, tel: 01248 353248. From April 1994 will be integrated into the Arts Council of Wales.

North West Arts Board, 4th Floor, 12 Harter Street, Manchester, M1 6HY, tel: 0161 228 3062. Covers Cheshire, Greater Manchester, Lancashire, Merseyside and High Peak District of Derbyshire.

Northern Arts Board, 9/10 Osborne Terrace, Newcastle upon Tyne, NE2 1NZ, tel: 0191 281 6334. Covers Cleveland, Cumbria, Durham, Northumberland and Tyne & Wear.

Scottish Arts Council, 12 Manor Place, Edinburgh, EH3 7DO, tel: 0131 226 6051. Covers visual arts and crafts in Scotland.

South East Arts Board, 10 Mount Ephraim, Tunbridge Wells, TN4 8AS, tel: 01892 515210. Covers Kent, Surrey and East & West Sussex, excluding Greater London areas.

South East Wales Arts Association, Victoria Street, Cwmbran, NP44 3YT, tel: 01633 875075. Covers Mid-Glamorgan, South Glamorgan, Gwent and South Powys. From April 1994 will be integrated into the Arts Council of Wales.

South West Arts Board, Bradninch Place, Gandy Street, Exeter, EX4 3LS, tel: 01392 218188. Covers Avon, Cornwall, Devon and Dorset (except Bournemouth, Christchurch and Poole areas), Gloucestershire and Somerset.

Southern Arts Board, 13 St Clements Street, Winchester, SO23 9UQ, tel: 01962 855099. Covers Berkshire, Buckinghamshire, Hampshire, Isle of Wight, Oxfordshire, Wiltshire, and the Poole, Bournemouth and Christchurch areas of Dorset.

Welsh Arts Council, Museum Place, Cardiff, CF1 3NX, tel: 01222 394711. Covers visual arts and crafts in Wales. From April 1994 becomes Arts Council of Wales.

West Midlands Arts Board, 82 Granville Street, Birmingham, B1 2LH, tel: 0121 631 3121. Covers Hereford & Worcester, Shropshire, Staffordshire, Warwickshire and West Midlands.

West Wales Arts Association, 3 Red Street, Carmarthen, Dyfed, SA31 1QL, tel: 01267 234248. Covers West Glamorgan and Dyfed.
From April 1994, will be integrated into the Arts Council of Wales.

Yorkshire and Humberside Arts Board, 21 Bond Street, Dewsbury, WF13 1AX, tel: 01924 455555, fax: 0924 466522. Covers Humberside and North, South & West Yorkshire.

Grants and Advice

British Council, 11 Portland Place, London, W1N 4EJ, tel: 0171 930 8406. Provides contact with 90 countries through 162 offices abroad where funds may be available to assist in-coming artists. May provide some help to artists with firm invitations to exhibit abroad. Leaflet *Studying Abroad* (from Education Information Centre, 10 Spring Gardens, London SW1A 2BN), briefly describes schemes they administer.

Calouste Gulbenkian Foundation, 98 Portland Place, London, W1N 4ET, tel: 0171 636 5313, fax: 0171 636 2948. New Horizons Artist's Bursaries, offered in 1992 and 1993, are designed to help experienced artists (writers, performing, media and visual artists) work in a new art form.

Central Bureau for Educational Visits and Exchanges, Seymour Mews House, Seymour Mews, London, W1H 9PE, tel: 0171 486 5101, fax: 0171 935 5741. Grant and bursary schemes to encourage study abroad and co-operation in education. Young Workers Exchange Programme and Youth for Europe also organised.

David Canter Memorial Trust,
PO Box 3, Ashburton, Devon, TQ13 7UW.
Annual awards to makers for travel or special projects.

Erasmus, 15 rue d'Arlon, 1040 Brussels, Belgium, tel: [00 32] 2 233 0111. Grants for academic staff to undertake temporary teaching assignments in EC universities including travel grants for making contacts in other countries. Exchanges of between 3 months and a year.

European Pepinieres for Young People, 3 rue Debelleyme, 75003 Paris, France, tel: [00 33] 1 48 04 78 79, contact: Pierre Keryvin. Has offered 3-6 month residencies with workspace, accommodation and living expenses to artists in various artistic disciplines in European cities. Short-list decided by national panel, final candidates by international jury.

Foundation for Sport and the Arts,
PO Box 20, Liverpool, L9 6EA, tel: 0151 524 0235, fax: 0151 524 0285.

German Academic Exchange Service (DAAD), 2 Bloomsbury Square, London, WC1A 2LP, tel: 0171 404 4065. Offers study visits, scholarships and research grants in various categories.

ICOM (Industrial Common Ownership Movement), Vassalli House, 20 Central Road, Leeds, LS1 6DE, tel: 0113 246 1738. Has replaced the Co-operative Development Agency as provider of advice on setting up workers' co-ops. Can provide contacts with local agencies.

Kaleidoscope, Commission of the European Communities, UK Office, 8 Storey's Gate, London, SW1P 3AT. Annual awards with changing categories, covering all artforms to support cultural events which involve at least three European partners. Deadline for 1994 was 1 December 1993.

Kathleen and Margery Elliott Scholarships, 10 Bennett Hill, Birmingham, B2 5RS, contact: B Flint LLB. Educational exchange grants including maintenance and travel for projects which have already gained some funding.

Kunstlerhaus Bethanien, Mariennenplatz 2, 1000 Berlin 36, Germany. International arts centre with workshops and studios for invited artists, average visit 6–12 months.

LEDU, LEDU House, Upper Galwally, Belfast, BT8 4TB, tel: 01232 491031. Provides advice and training for small businesses in N Ireland.

Marks & Spencer, Michael House, Baker Street, London, W1A 1DN, tel: 0171 935 4422, contact: Elizabeth Callender (Community Affairs Manager).

Prince's Trust, 8 Bedford Row, London, WC1R 4BA, tel: 0171 405 5799, contact: Anne Engel. Offers schemes which assist young people (under 25, or under 29 if disabled) to make contacts in Europe including Richard Mills Travel Fellowships, Go and See, Go Ahead and European Vision.

Prince's Youth Business Trust, 5th Floor, 5 Cleveland Place, London, SW1Y 6JJ, tel: 0171 321 6500, fax: 0171 834 6494. Helps designers and artists between the ages of 18-29 to set up in business, providing financial advice and grants and loans of up to £5000.

Rural Development Commission, 141 Castle Street, Salisbury, SP1 3TP, tel: 01722 336255. Can provide addresses of local offices which may offer capital grants towards conversion of redundant buildings in rural areas.

St Hugh's Foundation, Andrew & Co (Solicitors), St Swithin's Square, Lincoln, LN2 1HB. Promotes innovation, research and education in the arts, giving travel bursaries, scholarships and fellowships to individuals and organisations in the Lincolnshire and Humberside areas.

Training and Enterprise Councils (TECs). See telephone directory for local details. Advice, information and training on a business set-up and development. For Scotland, contact Local Enterprise Councils and Northern Ireland, Local Enterprise Development Unit.

Information

ABSA, Nutmeg House, 60 Gainsford St, Butlers Wharf, London, SE1 2NY, tel: 0171 378 8143, fax: 0171 407 7527. Provides information for businesses to encourage sponsorship of the arts, and administers the Business Sponsorship Incentive Scheme. Other offices are: **ABSA Northern England**, Dean Clough, Halifax, W Yorks, HX3 5AX, tel: 01422 344555. **ABSA Northern Ireland**, 181A Stranmillis Road, Belfast, BT9 5BU, tel: 01232 664736, fax: 01232 661715. **ABSA Scotland**, Room 206, West Port House, 102 West Port, Edinburgh, EH93 9HS, tel: 0131 228 4262, fax: 0131 229 9008. **ABSA Wales**, 9 Museum Place, Cardiff, CF1 3NX, tel: 01222 221382.

Action Resource Centre, 102 Park Village East, London, NW1 3SP, tel: 0171 383 2200. Encourages companies to offer in-kind support including staff secondments. Regional offices: Avon 01275 394040; Bradford 01274 484030; Derby 01332 364784; London 0171 383 2200; Manchester 0161 236 3391; Leeds 0113 237 0777; Leicester 0116 254 3398; Merseyside 0151 708 9929; Nottingham 0115 947 0749; Tower Hamlets 0171 375 0259; W Midlands 0121 643 9998; Scotland 0131 334 9876.

Action with Communities in Rural England (ACRE), Somerford Court, Somerford Road, Cirencester, GL7 1TW, tel: 01285 653477. Can provide a list of Rural Community Councils who may be able to offer advice to projects in rural areas.

Association of Commonwealth Universities, John Foster House, 36 Gordon Square, London, WC1H 0PF, tel: 0171 387 8572. Offers a publication and information service through small reference library (appointment necessary); can offer advice on awards, fellowships and scholarships.

Association of Visual Artists in Wales, Arts Workshop Gallery, Gloucester Place, Maritime Quarter, Swansea, tel: 01792 652016. Representative body for artists in Wales.

British American Arts Association, 116 Commercial Street, London, E1 6NF, tel: 0171 247 5385. Information resource to aid professional artists to work in US and develop links and exchanges in Europe. Reference library open to personal callers.

Business in the Arts, ABSA, 60 Gainsford Street, Butler's Wharf, London, SE1 2NY, tel: 0171 378 8143, fax: 0171 407 7527. Encourages business people to help arts managers through offering training, links with enterprise agencies and placements. See regional independent offices below.

Business in the Arts East Midlands, Mountfields House, Forest Road, Loughborough, LE11 3HU, tel: 01509 265 580, fax: 01509 262 214. **Business in the Arts Milton Keynes**, PO Box 23, Civic Offices, Milton Keynes, MK9 3YN, tel: 01908 682698, fax: 01908 682290. **Business in the Arts North**, Tyne & Wear Foundation, Mea House, Ellison Place, Newcastle upon Tyne, NE1 8XS, tel: 0191 222 0945, fax: 0191 230 0689. **Business in the Arts North West**, 59 Rodney Street, Liverpool, L1 9ER, tel: 0151 709 8780, fax: 0151 707 0758. **Business in the Arts Scotland**, c/o Royal Bank of Scotland, Dale House, 21 West George Street, Glasgow, G2 1EW, tel: 0141 204 3864, fax: 0141 204 3897. **Business in the Arts South**, c/o Southampton Institute of Higher Education, East Park Terrace, Southampton, SO9 4WW, tel: 01703 335311, fax: 01703 222259. **West Midlands Business in the Arts**, 82 Granville Street, Birmingham, B1 2LH, tel: 0121 631 3121, fax: 0121 643 7239. **Business in the Arts Yorkshire & Humberside**, Dean Clough Office Park, Halifax, HX3 5AX, tel: 01422 345631, fax: 01422 367860.

CAFE (Creative Activity for Everyone), 23/25 Moss Street, Dublin 2, tel: [00 353] 1 677 0330. Information resource holding lists of creative people across Ireland, organisations, resources and exhibition spaces. Produces *Funding Handbook* and newsletter.

Careers Services. Careers Service Units in higher and further education institutions provide information and advice to current and ex-students and access to all major reference books on grants, awards and scholarships.

Centre for European Business Information, Small Firms Service, 11 Belgrave Road, London, SW1V 1RB, tel: 0171 828 6201. Free information pack and details of other centres.

Charities Aid Foundation, 48 Pembury Road, Tonbridge, Kent, TN9 2JD, tel: 01732 771 333. Promotes charitable giving.

Charity Commission, St Albans House, 57-60 Haymarket, London, SW1Y 4QX, tel: 0171 210 3000, fax: 0171 930 9173. Deals with applications for charity status.

Commission of the European Communities, Jean Monnet House, 8 Storey's Gate, London, SW1P 3AT, tel: 0171 973 1992, fax: 0171 973 1900. Information service including details of institutions, study and courses in EC countries open to visitors between 10-1pm daily and for telephone queries 2-5pm.

Directory of Social Change, 24 Stephenson Way, London NW1 2DP, tel 0171 209 5151. Publisher of information for the voluntary sector; also runs national training courses (topics include fundraising) for charities and voluntary organisations. **Northern office:** Federation House, Hope Street, Liverpool L1 tel 0151 708 0117.

DTI (Department of Trade & Industry). Tel: 0181 200 1992. Provides information to help British businesses compete in UK, Europe and elsewhere. Regional offices: **East** 01245 492385; **E Midlands** 0115 950 6181; **N East** 0191 232 4722; **N West** 0151 227 4111; **N Ireland** 01232 233 3233; **S East** 0171 215 0538/0541, 01737 226900, 01734 395600; **Scotland** 0141 248 2855; **S West** 0117 927 2666; **Wales** 01222 825111; **W Midlands** 0121 212 5000; **Yorks & Humbs** 01532 443171.

Euro Information Centres. Information on legislation, EC research/development programmes, law, grants/loans, etc; contacts, trade fairs, etc. **Belfast** 01232 491031; **Birmingham** 0121 454 6171; **Bradford** 01274 752462; **Brighton** 01273 220870; **Bristol** 0117 973 7373; **Cardiff** 01222 229525; **Exeter** 01392 214085; **Glasgow** 0141 221 0999; **Inverness** 01464 234121; **Leeds** 0113 243 9222; **Leicester** 0116 255 4464; **Liverpool** 0151 298 1928; **London** 0171 261 1163/ 489 1992; **Maidstone** 01622 694109; **Manchester** 0161 236 3210; **Newcastle** 0191 261 0026; **Norwich** 01603 625977; **Nottingham** 0115 962 4624; **Slough** 01753 577 8777; **Telford** 01952 588766; **Southampton** 01703 832866; **Stafford** 01785 59528.

Federation of Charity Advice Services. Members can provide information and advice to voluntary organisations (rather than individuals). Some offices offer access to FunderFinder, a computerised database of over 1000 trusts. Offices at: **Cleveland** 01642 240651; **Coventry** 01203 220381; **Derbyshire** 0162 982 4797; **Dorset** 01305 205059; **Hampshire** 01962 854971; **Hereford & Worcester** 01684 573334; **Hounslow** 0181 577 3226; **Lancashire** 01772 718710; **Newcastle** 0191 232 7445; **Norfolk** 01953 851408; **North East** 0191 477 1253; **N Ireland** 01232 321224; **Nottingham** 0602 476614; **Reading** 01491 39766 ext 29; **S Yorks** 0114 276 5460; **Somerset** 01823 217353; **Stafford** 01785 42525; **Suffolk** 01473 230000; **Sussex** 01273 21398; **Wales** 01222 869224; **W Midlands** 0121 643 8477; **W Yorks** 01924 382120; **Wiltshire** 01380 729279.

IRIS, Equal Opportunities Unit, Employment Department, c/o SNHS 2, Porter Brook House, Moorfoot, Sheffield, S1 4PQ, tel: 0114 259 7567. Promotes and supports the exchange of experience concerning vocational training for women. Finance available for exchanges between training programmes for women and other projects which disseminate information.

Minorities Arts Advisory Service, 4th Floor, 28 Shacklewell Lane, London, E8 2EZ, tel: 0171 254 7295. Offers information and training for artists and artists groups on topics including fundraising.

National Artists Association (NAA), Spitalfields, 21 Steward Street, London E1 6AJ, tel 0171 426 0911, fax 0171 426 0282. Offers advice and information through conferences, publications and other activities.

National Council for Voluntary Organisations, Regent's Wharf, 8 All Saints Street, London, N1 9RL, tel: 0171 713 6161, fax: 0171 713 6300. Information on sources of help and funding for voluntary organisations.

Northern Ireland Council for Voluntary Organisations, 127 Ormeau Road, Belfast, BT7 1SH, tel: 01232 321224. National body for the voluntary sector in N Ireland.

PETRA, Central Bureau of Educational Visits and Exchanges, Seymour Mews, London, W1H 9PE, tel: 0171 486 5101, fax: 0171 935 5741. Aims to raise standards and the quality of technical and vocational education, stimulate trans-national co-operations and partnerships and promote European training. Encourages exchanges and work placements in Europe for young people.

Scottish Council for Voluntary Organisations, 18/19 Claremont Crescent, Edinburgh, EH7 4QD, tel: 0131 556 3882, fax: 0131 556 0279. Information and publications for voluntary organisations in Scotland.
See 'Further reading'.

Wales Council for Voluntary Action, Llys Ifor, Crescent Road, Caerphilly, Mid-Glamorgan, CF8 1XL, tel: 01222 869224, fax: 01222 860627. Information and publications for voluntary organisations in Wales.

Training

AMTIS (Arts Management Training Initiative Scotland), Moray house Institute, Chessel's Land, Holyrood Road, Edinburgh EH8 8AQ, tel 0131 558 6506. Training courses for visual artists, craftspoeple and adminstrators.

Arts Management Centre, 65 Westgate Road, Newcastle upon Tyne NE1 1SG, tel 0191 221 0419, fax 0191 261 7002. Short courses in arts management topics including marketing, fundraising, etc.

Arts Training Programme, School of Performing Arts, De Montfort University, Scraptoft Campus, Leicester, LE1 9BH, tel: 0116 257 7804. Short courses for artists and arts administrators in management topics including fundraising. Specialist courses for artists run in conjunction with East and West Midlands Arts.

Arts Training South, CCE, University of Sussex, Falmer, Brighton, BN1 9QH, tel: 01273 606755. Short courses, seminars and other training events.

Arts Training South West, Melville House, 12 Middle Street, Taunton, Somerset TA1 1SH, tel 01823 334767, fax 01823 334668.

Centre for Arts Management, Institute of Public Administration & Management, University of Liverpool, PO Box 147, Liverpool, L69 3BX, tel: 0151 794 2916. Short courses for arts administrators and artists in management topics including fundraising.

Interchange Training, Interchange Studios, Dalby Street, London, NW5 3NQ, tel: 0171 267 5220, contact: 0171 482 5292. Courses include Fundraising in the Arts and Fundraising for Voluntary Organisations.

NACVS (National Association of Councils for Voluntary Service), 3rd Floor, Arundel Court, 177 Arundel Gate, Sheffield, SI2 NU, tel 01742 786636. Co-ordinates programme of courses run by local CVS and ofter training bodies aimed at small voluntary organisations.

The writers

Brian Baker is a free-lance journalist writing for *Artists Newsletter, Stage & Television Today, Arts Management Weekly, Museums Journal* and *Public Service Local Government.*

Eddie Chambers is a freelance curator associated with the Institute of New International Visual Arts.

Lee Corner is a free-lance writer and researcher in the arts. Recent work includes researching the Code of Practice for the Visual Arts for the National Artists Association.

Yvonne Deane is Chief Executive of Axis – visual arts information service.

Susan Foster is an arts administrator and former co-ordinator of the Oxfordshire Visual Arts Week.

Susan Jones is an artist. She also undertakes visual arts research for arts boards and other bodies, and in 1992 edited the AN Publications book *Art in Public.* Since 1987, she has been News Editor of *Artists Newsletter.*

Maureen Mackin of the Belfast-based organisation Mackin Robinson Art Services, provides project management, research and consultancy for the arts.

Simon Pallett is a Chartered Accountant and a Lecturer in Accounting and Finance in the School of Business Management at the University of Newcastle upon Tyne. Previously he worked for Northern Arts Board as Assistant Director (Finance and Administration).

Helen Smith is an artist who has initiated education, public art and exhibition projects.

Index

Index

Artists Handbooks

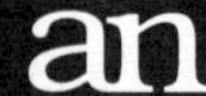

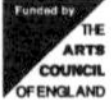

)rganising Your Exhibition

ull of sound, practical advice on all aspects of exhibition organisation and an ideal ompanion to Investigating Galleries, it offers an instant solution to the agonies of rganising a show. Covering everything from showing in alternative spaces to the ols needed to get a show up and from how to locate spaces and selling the work, it ven tells you how to estimate the wine needed for the private view!

ebbie Duffin, PB, A5, 116pp, ISBN 0 907730 14 0, £7.25

laking Ways

ne visual artists' guide to surviving and thriving

uite apart from helping artists, makers and photographers to grapple with the athsome necessities of exhibiting, selling, self-employment, planning work, etc, this ook offers plenty of sound, witty and inspiring advice on how to actually thrive. As ell as covering the myriad of ways visual artists can get involved in community-ased work, it also has chapters on health and safety, benefits, copyright and financial dministration. There is little that practitioners need to know which isn't included here.

d. David Butler, PB, A5, 256pp, illus, ISBN 0 907730 16 7, £11.99

\rt in Public

vhat, why and how

n intelligent guide to the complex theoretical and practical issues affecting art in ublic, a field of work which includes both the infamous 'turd in the plaza' and the enuinely popular and imaginative initiatives which transform and revitalise public paces. *Art in Public* provides a thought-provoking account of the values and hilosophies which give rise to the range work and debates their implications for art, ne artist and the public. Commissioners, agencies and artist have found this an nvaluable reference, and even artists, makers and photographers with no intention of going public' at present will find this a stimulating introduction to debate which is set) run and run.

d. Susan Jones, PB, 178pp, illus, ISBN 0 907730 18 3, £9.95

Exhibiting & Selling Abroad

ndoubtedly one of our most successful publications, this book provides food for nought for all artists, makers and photographers who are developing an international erspective. Covering everything from exhibitions and trade fairs to residencies and stu-io visits, *Exhibiting & Selling Abroad* combines the inspiration which comes from eading about artists' own experiences with highly practical information on exporting, ales administration and networking.

udith Staines, PB, A5, 120pp, illus, ISBN 0 907730 21 3, £7.25

Selling

'his should be compulsory reading for those artists who believe that if left to its own evices in studio, gallery or on top of the wardrobe, work will somehow contrive to sell self. *Selling* examines the ins and outs of selling and illustrates how artists, makers and hotographers have benefited from a more pro-active approach. It explains how to work ut prices and identify the best outlets, and looks in detail at the advantages and isadvantages of everything from trade fairs and agents to exhibitions and commissions.

udith Staines, PB, A5, 136pp, Illus, ISBN 0 907730 19 1, £7.25

Directory of Exhibition Spaces

Seeking to show? Fixing an exhibition tour? The *Directory of Exhibition Spaces* covers everything you need to know about galleries showing temporary programmes of contemporary visual arts, crafts, photography and live art performances. It lists over 2100 galleries and exhibition spaces – however large or small – in the UK and Ireland, describing art forms shown, exhibition policy and gallery space. Also includes access information for disabled visitors. To make it user-friendly for artists, exhibition organisers and visual arts professionals the directory has been indexed by arts funding region/county/ town as well as by gallery highlighting art forms shown, if applications are welcome and whether space is hired out.

Ed. Janet Ross, pub-lished end of JUNE 95, PB, 336pp, ISBN 0 907730 27 2, £13.99.

Artist Handbooks

Live Art

Designed for all visual artists whose work involves live or temporary activities, *Live Art* combines information about the aspirations and experiences of artists with the practical considerations of putting on an event. A useful guide for artists, promoters and curators.

Ed. Robert Ayers & David Butler, PB, A5, 178pp, illus, ISBN 0 907730 13 2, £7.25

Across Europe

the artist's guide to travel and work

Looks at 24 European countries through the eyes of artists who live there and UK artists who've lived, studied or worked there and in doing so, provides valuable insights into each country's cultural character and the practicalities of exhibiting, selling, creating opportunities and making contacts. Comes with a free copy of the *Artists & the EU* Fact Pack (worth £1.85) which covers artists' rights and responsibilities, sources of information and advice, and gives profiles of EU countries.

Ed. David Butler, PB, A5, 168pp, illus, ISBN 0 907730 15 9, £9.95

Money Matters

Problems with pricing? Baffled by book-keeping? Get Money Matters: the artist's financial guide and stop the headaches. Changes in how tax is calculated for self-employed people, and the introduction of self-assessment (working out your own tax bill) make it more important than ever for people running small businesses to have a good grasp of financial systems. This fully-revised second edition provides expert advice on taxation and the Inland Revenue, National Insurance, VAT, pricing work, and handling customers, suppliers and banks. And all this is backed-up with a model accounting system written especially for visual arts and crafts businesses.

Richard Murphy, Sarah Deeks & Sally Nolan, PB, 134pp, ISBN 0 907730 26 4, £7.25

Copyright

Expert advice about the applications of the 1988 Copyright, Designs & Patents Act, negotiating agreements, making sure you get the best from selling your copyright and how to deal with infringements. Contains practical examples of how artists, makers and photographers have dealt with copyright and reproduction issues.

Roland Miller, PB, A5, 125pp, illus, ISBN 0 907730 12 4, £7.25

Artists Newsletter

The monthly magazine providing analysis, commentary and information across contemporary visual arts practice.

ARTISTS & ARTWORK features review-based articles by curators, critics and artists commenting on what lies behind current practice. It covers exhibitions, installations, art in public, new media and issue-based projects. OUTLOOK is an illustrated round-up of new work, and WHAT'S ON is the monthly guide to temporary exhibitions and live art events around the country.

The **PRACTICAL PAGES** give comprehensive information on opportunities across the visual arts. Over 1000 are listed each year, including open exhibitions, gallery calls for applications, awards, residencies, commissions, mail-art, art and craft fairs and competitions. Features providing expert technical and business advice are run alongside the Help page, Small Ads, Sits Vac and the artists' contact page Pinboard.

In **ISSUES AND NEWS,** writers from the world of arts, education and politics map out the social, economic and political context for the arts, and in-depth articles are linked with short reports on issues.

Twelve issues a year, available from selected retail outlets at £2 a copy, or by mail-order subscription.

Individual ■ UK £19.95
■ Europe £28
■ Overseas £36

Institution ■ UK, Europe, Overseas £36

Prices quoted as at May 1995 are subject to alteration, please check before ordering.

Visual Arts Contracts

an

Introduction to Contracts

Designed to be read as the first step to making professional legal agreements, *Introduction to Contracts,* outlines the elements and terms you might find in a contract, and provides artists with the ammunition they need to negotiate, deal with disputes and find a suitable solicitor.

PB, A4, 12pp, £1.50

Residencies

Demystifies the legal arrangements for artists' residencies in any kind of settings. The ready-to-use contract form for a residency deals with having more than one partner in an agreement, and the workshop contract can be adapted for many 'one-off' activities. Also contains notes on employment and tax, copyright, moral and reproduction rights.

PB, A4, 20pp, ISBN 0 907730 25 6, £3.50

Commission Contracts

Maps out the legal arrangements necessary for all those who work with commissions and public art. By comparing public and private arrangements and describing the roles of parties in public art commissions, functions of agents and dealers and the implications of sub-contracting. Fill-in contract forms for Commissioned Design, Commission and Sale for Public Art and Private Commission Contract.

PB, A4, 20pp, £3.50

Licensing Reproductions

Make the most of your images by getting the licensing agreements right. This contract sets out how to grant or obtain permission to reproduce artwork or designs, and includes details of what licensing agreements to use, and notes on fees and royalties and negotiating and monitoring agreements.

PB, A4, 20pp, £3.50

NAA Public Exhibition Contract

The National Artists Association, commissioned this contract to cover the legal arrangements surrounding showing work in public galleries and exhibition spaces. Many artists, makers and photographers as well as galleries have found it an invaluable way to clarify responsibilities. It includes ready-to-use contract forms for a public exhibition and an exhibition tour, along with information on fees, selling, insurance and promotion.

PB, A4, 24pp, £3.50

Selling Contracts

If selling is part of your practice, then you need this contract. It deals exclusively with selling art and craft work and covers selling to private buyers, galleries and shops, and includes a contract form for selling on sale or return.

PB, A4, 14pp, £3.50

Developed because the visual arts profession needed effective agreements to cover all aspects of contemporary visual arts practice, our Visual Arts Contracts will ensure that collaborations between artists, exhibition organisers, agents, and commissioners are professional and harmonious. Written by Nicholas Sharp – a solicitor specialising in contract preparation and negotiation for business and the arts – they are legally sound, and contain either ready-to-fill-in forms or a point-by-point checklist with explanatory notes. Each comes with permission for the purchaser to make additional copies for their own professional use.

Ordering details

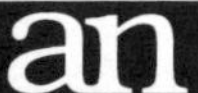

For mail orders add £1.50 per order for postage (UK), £2.50 per order (Europe), £4 per order (Overseas). Telephone credit card orders to 0191 514 3600 (Ref EI), or write to: AN Publications, PO Box 23, Sunderland SR4 6DG (prices quoted at May '95 are subject to change, please check before ordering).

Help us to improve our books

...help us stay in touch with your needs and interests by filling in and returning th freepost form. Your opinions are important and will help us to continue to publish th kinds of books you need, when you need them. To thank you for your help, we will ser you a discount voucher for use when purchasing other books from AN Publications.

Title of book ____________________

Where did you buy it? ____________________

Why did you choose it?

❑ Best coverage of the subject ❑ Recognised the author

❑ Recognised the publisher ❑ The price was right

❑ Other (please specify) ____________________

Where did you hear about this book?

❑ Book review in ____________________

❑ Leaflet in ____________________

❑ Advertisment in ____________________

❑ Browsing in ____________________ booksho

❑ Personal recommendation

❑ Other (please specify) ____________________

Have you any comments on the content of this book?

Name Address

Postcode Tel

Send to: Abigail Frazer, AN Publications, Freepost, PO Box 23, Sunderland, SR1 1BR. Tel 091 567 3589

Thank you for taking the time to fill in this form. Where shall we send your voucher?